PEGGY
HUTCHINSON'S
HOME MADE
WINE SECRETS

Revised by W. H. Crabtree

LONDON
W. FOULSHAM & CO. LTD.
NEW YORK : TORONTO : CAPE TOWN : SYDNEY

W. FOULSHAM & CO. LTD.,
Yeovil Road, Slough, Berks, England.
ISBN 0–572–00004–9

Printed in England by
The Camelot Press Ltd, Southampton

PREFACE TO PEGGY HUTCHINSON'S EARLIER REVISION

The recipes in this book were originally compiled in the days of plenty before the Second World War. Times have changed; some of the ingredients are no longer easy to obtain, and prices have increased. Yet when I came to revise the book I found that it needed less alteration than I had feared. Apart from a few minor alterations I was able to leave the recipes in their original form. All that I have had to rewrite is the introductory chapter, "General Hints on Wine Making." I have modified this to take into account the changed conditions, and at the end of it will be found advice on the use of substitutes for ingredients that are not easily obtainable.

The purpose of the book remains the same as when it was written. My aim has been true thrift – namely, getting the best from easily obtained ingredients. By this means we can revive traditional old English hospitality, when wine and cakes were served to all callers, and housewives treasured their particular recipes and vied with one another in the excellency of their brews.

PEGGY HUTCHINSON

PREFACE TO THIS REVISED EDITION

Peggy Hutchinson is famed for her traditional English winemaking recipes. As a farmer's wife she had ready access to the produce of the land, from garden, hedgerow and field and she used her journalistic talents to pass on her acquired knowledge and skills to a vast number of eager readers. This occurred both before and immediately following the Second World War, and as a consequence she discovered by experiment when and where suitable alternatives were acceptable.

For this new edition the recipes have been revised to take account of new techniques and the ready availability of modern wine-making equipment and materials. All the recipes have been metricated and for convenience both the British and Metric Measures are shown. In spite of all the changes, the recipes remain substantially the same as in the original edition – those of country housewife whose kitchen was her workshop and all nature a generous supplier of the main ingredients of her wines.

W. H. CRABTREE

CONTENTS

The Recipes are arranged Alphabetically.

GENERAL HINTS ON WINE MAKING

The word "wine" conjures up in one's mind a vision of vats, barrels, and cool cellars, all of which make wine making seem a very elaborate undertaking. But wine making in the home is easy. With inexpensive materials, simple equipment, and very little trouble, the average housewife can make good, fine English wine.

The garden and hedgerow provide a multitude of fragrant blooms and berries that will yield a gallon of delightful wine for less than the price of a single bottle of the cheapest wine in the shops. The range of types and flavours is wide and many of the ingredients cost nothing at all.

The most important ingredient of all is *time,* and that costs nothing but patience. For wine makes itself.

The main qualities to aim at in wine making are flavour, body, clearness, and colour. There are a number of different methods of wine making, and these can be put under four general headings:

(1) The cold water method.
(2) The boiling water and boiling method.
(3) The pure juice method.
(4) The diluted juice method.

The recipes in this book include examples of all of these methods. I have given the most suitable method for each wine.

UTENSILS

It is advisable in wine making to use utensils that are made of plastic material, glass or porcelain and kept solely for that purpose. This is because wine very easily takes on undesirable flavours. Above all, metal containers should never be employed. They really do ruin the flavour of the finished product.

First of all it will be necessary to obtain a high density plastic bucket in which to make the brew. These are normally made to hold 9 litres (2 gallons) when filled to the brim, and will comfortably contain the $4\frac{1}{2}$ litres (1 gallon) which is the usual quantity made at one time. A sheet of polythene large enough to cover the top of the bucket and capable of being tied under the rim will also be needed.

The second stage of the process calls for a large glass 4½ litre (1 gallon) fermentation jar, sometimes called a demijohn. This can be obtained from health stores and chemists which deal with wine making equipment. At the same time purchase a one-holed rubber cork to fit the jar and a plastic air-lock. This allows the fermentation to take place in the absence of air and without the cork constantly being blown out.

The wine is left in the fermentation jar to clear and mature and is finally transferred to wine bottles fitted with clean, new corks. Wine bottles for this purpose can be purchased, but so many hotels and restaurants throw away hundreds every week that it is not difficult to find a manager who can be persuaded to let you have as many as you need. Make sure however that the bottles you obtain are indeed wine bottles since they are made of thicker glass than spirit bottles. The latter never have to withstand pressures built up by a further fermentation inside the bottle, but wine sometimes does start working again. The thicker glass prevents the bottle from bursting and hopefully the cork will fly out out first.

Whatever utensils you use, it is most important that you should keep them in good condition.

Never put wine in wet bottles. After washing out thoroughly with hot soda water, rinse them well in cold water and then put them in the oven and bake them until they are completely dry inside.

Don't let sediment lie at the bottom of wine bottles. This ruins the flavour. The process involving the removal of the clearer part from the heavy deposit (the lees) which settles at the bottom is called racking. It is done with a siphon so that the lees are disturbed as little as possible.

INGREDIENTS

Making good wine is so simple, and requires so little in the way of ingredients. You can make strong and invigorating brews from blooms, berries, leaves, and even waste. There is a very wide range for you to choose from, and all you have to do is to make your choice.

In wines as in everything else, one man's meat is another man's poison; and when you are making wine you must study your family's taste. On no account become a one-flavour wine maker. Suit the popular taste for sweetness, and give variety.

Caution is needed when you make up a wine recipe for yourself, and it is wise to consider carefully the distinct properties of various flowers and fruits, keeping a watchful eye on the strength of flavour.

As a rule you can class flowers up generally in your mind. Any strong-smelling flower will yield good results, excepting poppies and deadly nightshade. These flowers are harmful, as most country people know.

Flower heads and petals make the choicest wine. I find the stalks too strong and harsh. I like the flower heads best as the little green that goes with them produces an exquisite greeny-yellow colour that is truly delightful in primrose and cowslip. But you must be very careful in gauging quantities, as some flowers are harsh in flavour, and so rather less bulk of flower must go to the gallon.

Berries and fruit give the best colour when taken as soon as they are ripe. Those that have been hung through sunshine and rain have lots of moisture, but no colour and no flavour. All wines from such things as plums and brambles are nicer when leaning to red, and this is only obtained by keeping a wary eye on the season.

Some fascinating mixtures can be got by putting a later fruit to an earlier variety, or by putting two or several together, after making or in the making.

Certain shrubs and herbs make fine, sparkling wine such as rosemary, balm, mint and sage, when newly sprouted in the spring. After that they are too strong and make up bitterly.

Dried fruits also make fine wine, and are economical, as the fruit can be eaten; for there is no mashing done in the tub, only the liquor being fermented.

Almost everything can be made into good wine, including cabbage, turnips, and waste. Waste is an excellent wine maker – by this I mean orange skins and halves of lemons after being squeezed; apple cores and peelings, and windfall and bad apples (those with brown patches on them); small potatoes; lettuce and spinach leaves (the coarse ones); the hard blackberries, the poor-quality gooseberries and currants; little wizened, tough carrots, beets, and parsnips; unripened grapes from a cold greenhouse, and even the leaves of grapevines and the oak, and spring leaf-buds from the elder and bramble. All of these will make a good, nourishing brew. So will left-overs from meals – a cupful of rice pudding, a cupful of mashed potatoes, a few sultanas and two quarts of water with 0.7 kg (1½ lb.) of golden syrup will make a wine fit for a king! Marrow leaves and peelings and seeds, little tomatoes, mint, and the cores and skins of pears left when bottling fruit, all make excellent strong, drinkable wines. The list is almost endless.

ADDITIONAL INGREDIENTS

Seasoned drinkers like to feel a tingling heat in their fingers and toes. You can get a whisky-like quality in heat by adding whole cloves, whole ginger, peppercorns, or mustard seeds; you must wash them before adding. For a time you have the clove, ginger, pepper or mustard flavour; but it goes as the wine is kept, leaving only the tingling heat in the brew. Ginger in the bottle keeps the wine and improves its heat every day. Allow not more than 125 gm ($\frac{1}{4}$ lb.) to the gallon; 30 gm (1 oz.) is the wiser amount.

I find that whole cloves are better than ground cloves, which give a too pronounced taste. Whole cloves give heat with only a slight flavour, and in certain wines and syrups this is valuable for use as a nightcap for colds. A very fine wine is made solely with one ounce of cloves.

I do not advise stick cinnamon to flavour.

Malt, hops, barley, and wheat are all powerful additions to the brew, but these can be just as powerful an agent for ill in the hands of ignorance, for the bitterness of too many hops has to be tasted before it can be believed. Barley needs to be used with care. Barley wine has no harshness in making — it has a smooth, milk-like quality — but must be taken with care for it is deceptively mild to taste. The barley such as used to be ground for pigs and fed whole to hens cannot be obtained now, so you must be satisfied with pearl barley — that is, dressed barley from the shops.

There are other things that can be added that will make a big improvement, such as grape leaves, Indian corn, raisins, sultanas, and the peelings of oranges, lemons, and apples. Banana skins also give a fine flavour.

Finally, a necessary ingredient for all wines is tannin. Just as vegetables cooked without salt are insipid, so is wine without tannin. Tannin gives wine a bite, zest or character. Occasionally tannin will already be present in the materials from which the wine is made, but more often than not it will be necessary to add it. Buy wine tannin and put it in the brew at the rate stated on the bottle.

Before you start experimenting, first learn to make wine from the recipes as I have given them. If you throw a recipe out of balance you may find that you have wasted your ingredients.

MAKING THE WINE

If once you can fix a general rule in your head for wines, light, medium, and heavy, irrespective of kind, you will see just how easy a brew is to put together.

For a light wine use 1.4 kg (3 lbs.) to 1.8 kg (4 lbs.) of fruit and 1 litre (1 quart) of petals to 4½ litres (1 gallon).

For a medium flower wine use 2.25 litres (½ gallon) of petals and in the case of fruit wine 2.8 kg (6 lbs.) of fruit will produce 4½ litres (1 gallon) with a good bouquet and considerable strength.

For a heavy fruit wine as much as 3.6 kg (8 lbs.) of fruit can be used.

Decide just the kind you want, and work accordingly.

In all wine-making, and at every stage from beginning to end, extreme care must be taken to sterilize all the equipment used. Wine in the making is a ready prey for the vinegar fly which by its attentions can turn the whole brew to vinegar. To prevent this keep the wine covered closely all the time and wash out every piece of equipment to be used with a sterilising solution of sodium metabisulphite. Make this by dissolving 14 gm (½ oz.) of the powder in 1 litre (2 pints) of cold water. You can keep this solution in a plastic bottle and use it time and again for sterilising your buckets, jars and bottles.

To stir, mash and squeeze the fruit, I use my hand. This method is safer, cutting out all possibility of leaving the spoon resting at the side while you move something to make room on the shelf, and later find that the spoon slipped under the fruit and has been in the brew for days, completely spoiling the fine flavour the wine ought to have had.

Good colour is important. Bear in mind that boiling water will set a red but rob a yellow. Boiling water will rob certain kinds of wine of all distinctive properties, scent as well as colour, whereas cold water will preserve both.

Another hazard when using boiling water, and more-so when ingredients are boiled is the release of pectin. The latter is useful to the jam-maker since it is the pectin released in boiling that eventually sets the jam. Far from benefitting the wine-maker pectin is a nuisance and can produce a stubbornly cloudy wine. The solution is to use a pectin

11

destroying agent in all wines using boiling water in the making. The agent goes under various trade names such as Pectolase, Pectozyme or Pectolytic Enzyme. Use it as directed on the packet, adding it at the steeping stage.

Common sense and seasonal considerations must be taken into calculation. The period of mashing depends on the weather, for on hot, muggy days the fruits mould easily in the mash. To prevent early moulding of the mixture add two crushed Campden tablets when the brew is made. This will help to keep mould at bay for a few extra days whilst colour and flavour are being extracted. All mould should be taken off daily, and any sign of deterioration of fruit, leaf or flower is a signal for its removal. It is often quite easy to squeeze out the offending ingredient without disturbing the whole brew. On the other hand, never remove fruit or flower until you have got every particle of juice and flavour out of it, even if the recipe says only "stand ten days". If the mash is very fresh, I squeeze and push the fruit down for eighteen days and more, until I feel absolutely sure that I have got all the goodness into the liquor.

Some seasons the fruit is very soft, and quickly dissolves into the liquid; but very dry years usually mean that fruits like plums and cherries take three days to swell with the water. Flowerlets float on top and are easily skimmed off if you think they have given all their flavour.

Vine leaves must not be left in until they rot, although one summer I had them mixed with gooseberries for over a month.

Keep a book and write down the date of each brew and all the peculiarities it developed in the making, and this will guide you in the future and finally become invaluable. Using the same fruit and the same recipe gives different results in different years. A wet season will give a syrupy thickness that will clear up with time and make a heavy "body". A fine, dry year gives a full-flavoured thin wine of beautiful colour – and a multitude of beetles that take a lot of shaking off the flowers before wetting!

Some of my plum port has become a thin, red ruby wine; another brew has been a heavy red wine; and yet a third has turned out the colour and taste of real port. I am still trying to decide which I like best. Yet the same kind of plum and the same method were used for all of them. This has happened time and time again, and it is one of the things that makes wine making so fascinating. I welcome this variety, for each of the brews has its own special virtues and is good to drink.

STRAINING LIQUIDS

Straining the wine properly is most important. Use a nylon sieve for coarse straining and a fine nylon bag for fine straining. It is often found advisable to put the wine first through the sieve and then the bag. Strain into a plastic bucket. The sieve rests comfortably on the top of the bucket for coarse straining. While the bag is being used, rest it in the bucket and clip part of the edge of the bag round the rim of the bucket with three or four clothes' pegs.

FERMENTATION

Fermentation is the process which results in the formation of alcohol. When yeast cells are fed with sugar they reproduce themselves and alcohol and carbon dioxide gas are formed. The former causes the spirit content to build to a maximum of about 15% by volume and the carbon dioxide bubbles away into the atmosphere. For fermentation to occur, not only must yeast and sugar be present but several other conditions must be satisfied. These conditions call particularly for correct temperature and acidity. As far as temperature is concerned that of a normal living room is required. More accurately the optimum range for correct fermentation is between $15°$ C ($60°$ f) and $24°$ C ($75°$ F). The second condition stems from the fact that the yeast requires a slightly acid solution for fermentation. This is achieved in most recipes by the addition of the juice of oranges and lemons or simply by putting in citric acid.

Some wines mature more quickly than others, a change taking place in the bottle every hour. You will see tiny little bubbles come up and break on the surface; that is quiet fermentation, and it goes on for months. It is this "working" that refines the wine and makes it so delicious in the finished bottle. If you find that your wine has no movement, then it is in too cold a place. It will not spoil, but it will stand still and not improve until it gets into a warmer temperature. So generally speaking, you must ferment in the kitchen, or in a room where there is a fire on daily, or in summertime. Don't let the brew fret, or, in other words, have a very slow fermentation. Hasten the process by moving the jar into a warmer position.

13

THE HYDROMETER

The hydrometer is an instrument for measuring the specific gravity of a liquid, which for convenience is placed in a float-jar. The reading is shown on a scale let into the stem of the hydrometer. In a dense liquid the instrument floats higher and registers a high specific gravity on the scale. In wine-making the hydrometer is used to evaluate the progress of the fermentation. When sugar is first added a gravity reading of about 100 will be recorded. As the fermentation proceeds and the sugar used, the reading falls until eventually a zero reading or less indicates that all the available sugar has been used and a dry wine will result.

SUGAR TO USE

Generally speaking I have found that most brews need about 1.3 kg (3 lbs.) of sugar to $4\frac{1}{2}$ litres (1 gallon). It should be remembered that some of the other ingredients in the wine may contain sugar, e.g. beetroot and very ripe fruit, and in such cases less sugar needs to be added. If a dry wine is desired try to aim at an initial hydrometer reading of 100 and as this is reduced during fermentation to something between 0 and −10 it will produce a dry wine with alcoholic strength of around 14% by volume or 24.5 proof. The use of a larger amount of sugar will tend to produce a sweeter, stronger product.

Remember however that it is usually advantageous to conclude with a dry wine. Further fermentation is unlikely and the wine can always be sweetened to taste before being drunk.

For the delightful pale wines, such as primrose and cowslip, I advise white sugar. Best Demerara will not help these; on the contrary, it spoils the fine, faint hint of green that should tinge the yellow. For brandy cocktail, too, white sugar is best. But the best Demerara definitely does help the heavy yellow kinds, like lemon, rhubarb, and all the port-like brews.

Dark barley sugar will help the colour. Some people add burnt sugar and black "spanish", but these must be used with the greatest caution. Always be very careful about making additions of any kind, for they may interfere with the flavour and ruin your wine.

Thick wine is made by boiling the sugar into the water for thirty minutes or an hour. You boil the quantity down, and when it is

14

lukewarm, add yeast. In summers when insects are in the fruit this is the best method to use with plums, apples, and brambles.

THE YEAST TO USE

Our forbears had little choice regarding the yeast to use for their wine-making. They could buy fresh yeast from the local baker's or chemist's and 21 gm ($\frac{3}{4}$ oz.) was sufficient to ferment 4$\frac{1}{2}$ litres (1 gallon) of wine. The yeast was creamed with half a teaspoonful of sugar and a drop of luke-warm water and put in a warm place. It was then stirred into the brew. Some wine-makers still prefer to use this live yeast, but the ready availability of dried yeasts has provided a more convenient and a very reliable way of starting a fermentation. Ordinary dried active yeast, suitable for bread and wine-making can be bought in 100 gm (3$\frac{1}{2}$ oz.) tins and will keep for many months if stored in a cool, dry place. Three level teaspoonsful should be creamed in the same manner as the baker's yeast and stirred into the brew. Also on the market now are special yeasts for wine-making and these are very reliable and easy to use. They can be simply stirred into the brew at the rate suggested on the packet. In order to promote a speedy and thorough fermentation, yeast nutrient can be added at the same time as the yeast. I strongly recommend the use of yeast nutrient. Use a level teaspoonful of the nutrient to each 4$\frac{1}{2}$ litres (1 gallon) of wine.

"TRICKS OF THE TRADE"

There are many "tricks of the trade" in wine making, and one of the most important things to remember is that wine should never be thrown away just because it tastes sour and crabbed.

I once made some redcurrant wine, and tasted the brew after a few months. It was very sour and crabbed — and, foolishly, I poured it out. By luck I overlooked two bottles, and found them three years later. The wine proved to be delightful! That was a lesson to me in the futility of trying to make wine without the most necessary ingredient — time.

The point is that some wines mature more quickly than others, and a change takes place every three months. Often a brew develops a crabbed sourness at three months when it is busy developing "body". Don't throw it out as soured on the impulse of the moment. It only needs time to break up the crabbedness and bring out the fullness in flavour and body. At six months the flavour will probably be harsh with the sourness gone, and at twelve months there will be a matured brew in the bottle.

Sometimes the breaking up of the crabbedness can be helped with the addition of a little dark barley sugar to the brew. For example, elder flower made with golden syrup at times develops a raw bite; a little crushed barley sugar or brown toffee 250 gm ($\frac{1}{2}$ lb.) to 4$\frac{1}{2}$ litres (1 gallon), improves both the colour and taste.

I find that some seasons there is an extra acidity content in the wine, and that it gives a tremendous "grip" in the taste which is not altogether aggreeable to the general palate. To counteract this fault I pull 125 gm ($\frac{1}{4}$ lb.) of large raisins apart and add to the bulk, this quantity to a gallon; but more or less can be added according to the strength of the "grip" in taste. Where I feel that the harshness is due to a lack of sweetness owing to all the sugar being converted into spirit, I add 125 gm ($\frac{1}{4}$ lb.) or more (as needed) of brown sugar candy or barley sugar, but not till the wine is six months old. This causes a mild fermentation. But remember that most wine is harsh for the first six months and needs keeping, to justify the colour, clearness, and flavour. Saccharine is valuable in breaking up crabbedness, but it is a thing to be used with great care. Do not add more than one or two saccharines to the pint; one and a half is the best measurement. Only use when the wine has been kept over a time. I often use it in bramble wine. Always crush the saccharine before adding, or, alternatively, use the sweetener in its liquid form.

According to the harshness of the wine, you may also have to heat a little wine and stir into it 250 gm ($\frac{1}{2}$ lb.) to 500 gm (1 lb.) of syrup, then adding this to the whole and stirring to mix it in. Then cork, and leave for a month in a warm place. When you add extra sweetening of any kind, always let the wine stand for one, two, or three months in a warm place. Then taste it, and you will see how it has improved to a fine, drinkable quality.

When rhubarb wine is too sharp of acidity, add two large raisins to each bottle. This mellows it down beautifully.

A brew that remains stultifyingly sweet, on the other hand, needs some addition to turn that sweetness into a fine spirit content. One two-inch-thick slice of bread put in and left in a gallon for a week will make a surprising difference.

16

CLEARING

I find it a waste of time trying to clear wine while it is still fermenting. This can easily be seen when you knock the bottle on the shelf. Tiny air bubbles run up the wine, as they do in lemonade.

As soon as fermentation ceases, most wines begin to clear of their own accord. The deposits collect on the bottom of the demijohn and it is as well to siphon off the clearer part from the heavy deposits to prevent the latter from tainting the wine. This should be done every few weeks and some wines, given time, will clear themselves in this way. Others however prove more stubborn and it then becomes necessary to use wine finings. These are readily available and are simply added to the wine at the rate stated on the packet. After a few days the wine will be sparkling clear. Allow the deposit to settle firmly on the bottom of the jar and then siphon off the clear part.

CORKING

As I have suggested earlier it is as well to leave the wine in the fermentation jar until it is more or less ready to drink. The chances of renewed fermentation are then possible but remote.

Always use new corks. Beware of screw-stoppered bottles, for they are liable to go off "bang," making a dreadful mess with broken glass, and liquor will be spattered over the walls. Corks are safer, as they will blow out and can be replaced without much loss and upset.

SUBSTITUTES

Since I first wrote this book, some of the ingredients have become difficult to obtain, and in the last few years I have been experimenting with substitutes.

I have found that good golden syrup or honey can be used instead of sugar. The quantity to be used depends on the wine, but in general golden syrup should be the same as for sugar. Honey is dear, and must be treated with respect. If too much is used you get a *flavour* and a potent brew which gives you a violent headache for days.

When I wrote this book wheat and barley were plentiful and cost only about a penny a pint. Now times have changed, and substitutes may be required. I have found that the best substitute for wheat is white bread. Use one two-inch slice of bread to a gallon. An alternative is wheat flakes or Shredded Wheat. Two Shredded Wheat cakes may be used for 500 gm (1 lb.) of wheat.

Barley may be used instead of wheat in certain recipes, but remember that it makes the wine mature more quickly. On no account use both barley and wheat, or you will throw the recipe out of balance.

You can boil pearl barley or rice in water for thirty to forty minutes, and then strain out and use the barley or rice for puddings. The water can be made into any kind of wine, and will give a potent brew.

Lemons, oranges, and sultanas are obtainable. Sultanas can be used instead of raisins. Dates and other dried fruits are admissible.

RECIPES FOR WINES

GENERAL NOTES

1. The recipes are arranged alphabetically.

2. Full instructions are given on preparing the brew up to the point of putting it to ferment. This is done in a plastic bucket, covered closely with a sheet of polythene and placed in a warm room.

3. The procedure thereafter is the same in every case:—

(a) Leave to ferment for 5-7 days.

(b) Strain through a fine nylon bag and place in a fermentation jar filling it to the shoulder only. Fit an airlock. Put spare wine-to-be in an ordinary wine bottle fitted with a cotton wool bung and return jar and bottle to warm place to continue the fermentation.

(c) In about 21 days rack off the clearer wine from the jar and bottle. Return it to the jar filling the latter this time to the neck — using tepid water to fill up if more liquid is required. Return the jar to a warm place.

(d) Every 8-10 weeks rack the wine and take a hydrometer reading. When the latter has fallen to zero or less the fermentation will cease. It is no longer necessary to maintain the temperature so the jar can be removed to a cooler place.

(e) The wine will probably clear itself in due course but after some months add wine finings if still cloudy.

ALMOND WINE (1)

Ingredients:

43 gm bitter almonds	1½ ozs. bitter almonds
0.5 kg raisins	1 lb. raisins
1.3 kg sugar	3 lbs. sugar
4.5 litres water	1 gall. water
3 lemons	3 lemons
Tannin, yeast nutrient and yeast	Tannin, yeast nutrient and yeast

Method:—

1. Chop the almonds and raisins and boil gently in the water for an hour. Strain and make up the liquid to 4.5 litres (1 gall.)

2. Add the sugar and stir it away. When luke-warm put in the juice and thinly-pared rinds of the lemons. Take a reading with the hydrometer.

3. Stir in the tannin, yeast nutrient and yeast and ferment.

ALMOND WINE (2)

Ingredients:—

1.7 kg rhubarb	4 lbs. rhubarb
250 gm sultanas	¼ lb. sultanas
2 large teaspoonsful of almond essence	2 large teaspoonsful of almond essence
1.3 kg sugar	3 lbs. sugar
4.5 litres water – cold	1 gall. water – cold
1 lemon	1 lemon
2 Campden tablets	2 Campden tablets
Tannin, yeast nutrient and yeast	Tannin, yeast nutrient and yeast

Method:—

1. Cut the rhubarb up small, cover with the water and put in the crushed Campden tablets. Leave for 7 days, stirring and squeezing every day.

2. Strain through the coarse and fine strainers, squeezing out as much of the liquid as possible.

3. Add the sugar, almond essence, juice and thinly pared rind of the lemon and the chopped sultanas. Take a hydrometer reading.

4. Stir in the tannin, yeast nutrient and the yeast and ferment.

APPLE AND BLAEBERRY (Bilberry or Whortleberry) WINE

Ingredients:—

1.7 kg apples	4 lbs. apples
(windfalls will do but they must be clean)	(windfalls will do but they must be clean)
1.7 kg blaeberries	4 lbs. blaeberries
250 gm raisins	½ lb. raisins
1.5 kg sugar	3½ lbs. sugar
4.5 litres cold water	1 gall cold water
2 Campden tablets	2 Campden tablets
Tannin, yeast nutrient and yeast	Tannin, yeast nutrient and yeast

Method:—

1. Cut up the apples (do not peel or core) and put them into a plastic bucket with the blaeberries and the crushed Campden tablets. Pour on the cold water and stir and squeeze daily for 8 days. Strain.

2. Add the chopped raisins and sugar. Stir well and take a hydrometer reading.

3. Put in the tannin, yeast nutrient and yeast and ferment.

APPLE PORT
(Very rich and strong)

Ingredients:—

3.5 kg apples	8 lbs. apples
2.7 kg blaeberries	6 lbs. blaeberries
2 kg sugar	4½ lbs. sugar
4.5 litres cold water	1 gall. cold water
2 Campden tablets	2 Campden tablets
Tannin, yeast nutrient and yeast	Tannin, yeast nutrient and yeast

Method:—

1. Cut the apples up small (do not peel or core) and put them with the blaeberries and crushed tablets into a plastic bucket with the cold water. Squeeze and stir every day for 10 days and then strain.

2. Put in the sugar and stir until it has dissolved. Take a hydrometer reading.

3. Add tannin, yeast nutrient and yeast and ferment.

APPLE SHERRY

Ingredients:—

2.7 kg apples (windfalls will do)	6 lbs. apples (windfalls will do)
1 kg dried apricots	2 lbs. dried apricots
0.5 kg raisins	1 lb. raisins
1.5 kg sugar	3½ lbs. sugar
4.5 litres water	1 gall. water
1 cake shredded wheat	1 cake shredded wheat
2 Campden tablets	2 Campden tablets
Tannin, yeast nutrient and yeast	Tannin, yeast nutrient and yeast

Method:—

1. Boil the apricots in the water until very tender, then strain off the liquid and use the apricots as food.

2. Cut up the apples including peel and core and pour on the apricot liquid. Add the crushed Campden tablets, squeeze and mash every day for 10 days and then strain.

3. Add the shredded wheat, chopped raisins and sugar. Stir the latter away and take a reading with the hydrometer.

4. Put in the tannin, yeast nutrient and yeast and ferment.

APPLE WINE

Ingredients:—

3.5 kg bruised apples	8 lbs. bruised apples
250 gm sultanas	½ lb. sultanas
125 gm crushed barley	¼ lb. crushed barley
1.5 kg brown sugar	3½ lbs. brown sugar
4.5 litres cold water	1 gall. cold water
2 Campden tablets	2 Campden tablets
Tannin, yeast nutrient and yeast	Tannin, yeast nutrient and yeast

Method:—

1. Cut the apples into small pieces. Add the chopped sultanas, and the crushed barley and Campden tablets. Pour over the cold water and leave to steep for about 10 days stirring daily.

2. Strain and stir in the sugar until dissolved. Take a reading with the hydrometer.

3. Add the tannin, yeast nutrient and yeast and ferment.

APRICOT WINE (1)

Ingredients:—

2.7 kg apricots	6 lbs. apricots
1.5 kg sugar	3½ lbs. sugar
4.5 litres cold water	1 gall. cold water
2 teaspoonsful citric acid	2 teaspoonsful citric acid
2 Campden tablets	2 Campden tablets
Tannin, yeast nutrient and yeast	Tannin, yeast nutrient and yeast

Method:—

1. Cover the fruit with water, put in the crushed Campden tablets, squeezing and stirring daily for 10 days.

2. Strain off the liquid and make up to 4½ litres (1 gall.). Add citric acid and sugar and take a hydrometer reading when the latter has dissolved.

3. Put in tannin, yeast nutrient and yeast and ferment.

APRICOT WINE (2)

Ingredients:—

1.7 kg apricots	4 lbs. apricots
0.5 kg raisins	1 lb. raisins
0.5 kg wheat	1 lb. wheat
1.5 kg sugar	3½ lbs. sugar
4.5 litres cold water	1 gall. cold water
2 teaspoonsful citric acid	2 teaspoonsful citric acid
2 Campden tablets	2 Campden tablets
Tannin, yeast nutrient and yeast	Tannin, yeast nutrient and yeast

Method:—

1. Cover the apricots with the cold water and add the crushed Campden tablets. Mash and stir for 10 days and then strain.

2. To the liquid add the chopped raisins, sugar and wheat. Stir well and take a reading with the hydrometer.

3. Add citric acid, tannin, yeast nutrient and yeast and ferment.

BARLEY WINE

Ingredients:—

0.5 kg barley (crushed)	1 lb. barley (crushed)
0.5 kg raisins	1 lb. raisins
0.5 kg old potatoes	1 lb. old potatoes
1.5 kg sugar	3½ lbs. sugar
4.5 litres hot water	1 gall. hot water
2 teaspoonsful citric acid	2 teaspoonsful citric acid
Tannin, yeast nutrient and yeast	Tannin, yeast nutrient and yeast

Merthod:—

1. Put the barley, chopped raisins and potatoes (not peeled but cut into small pieces) into a bucket. Pour over the hot water, add the sugar and stir until dissolved. Take a hydrometer reading.

2. When luke-warm, put in the citric acid, tannin, yeast nutrient and yeast and ferment. Strain after 10 days.

BEETROOT WINE (1)

Ingredients:—

1.7 kg beetroot	4 lbs. beetroot
0.5 kg wheat	1 lb. wheat
1.5 kg sugar	3½ lbs. sugar
4.5 litres water	1 gall water
2 teaspoonsful citric acid	2 teaspoonsful citric acid
Pectolytic Enzyme	Pectolytic Enzyme
Tannin, yeast nutrient and yeast	Tannin, yeast nutrient and yeast

Method:—

1. Boil the beetroot gently in the water until tender and pink. Strain the water off and allow it to cool.

2. Add Pectolytic Enzyme and leave for at least 24 hours.

3. Add the wheat and sugar and stir until the latter has all dissolved. Take a reading with the hydrometer.

4. Put in citric acid, tannin, yeast nutrient and yeast and ferment.

BEETROOT WINE (2)

Ingredients:—

1.3 kg beetroot	3 lbs. beetroot
1.3 kg parsnips	3 lbs. parsnips
125 gm large raisins	¼ lb. large raisins
1.5 kg sugar	3¼ lbs. sugar
4.5 litres water	1 gall. water
1 teaspoonful citric acid	1 teaspoonful citric acid
Pectolytic Enzyme	Pectolytic Enzyme
Tannin, yeast nutrient and yeast	Tannin, yeast nutrient and yeast

Method:—

1. Boil the beetroot in half the water until tender, then skin and use the beetroot.

2. Boil the parsnips in the remaining half of the water until tender. Strain and use them as a vegetable.

3. Unite the two liquids and allow to cool. Add Pectolytic ... 24 hours.

... ed raisins and the sugar. Stir in and take a

... acid, tannin, yeast nutrient and yeast and

es **Wine**

U don't buy the " bees."
They form naturally in the
re, made as follows—Boil
quarts of water and allow
ol. Place in a large jar or
with one cup of barley,
n the husk. Sweeten with
or syrup and flavour
ginger. Cover and leave
" bees " appear and move
in the bottle. Use some
wine every day, topping
e jar with boiled, cooled
and adding more sweet-
and flavour. Add more
from time to time.—H.
son, Colinton, Edin-

25

BEETROOT WINE (3)
(Hackthorpe)

Ingredients:—

1.7 kg beetroot	4 lbs. beetroot
1.5 kg sugar	3½ lbs. sugar
4.5 litres water	1 gall. water
Juice of 3 lemons	Juice of 3 lemons
8 cloves	8 cloves
Pectolytic Enzyme.	Pectolytic Enzyme
Tannin, yeast nutrient and yeast	Tannin, yeast nutrient and yeast

Method:—

1. Wash the the beetroot and cut up quickly into the water and boil for 20 minutes. Strain.

2. Allow to cool and add the Pectolytic Enzyme. Leave for 24 hours.

3. Put in the lemon juice, the sugar and the cloves. Stir well to dissolve the sugar then take a reading with the hydrometer.

4. Add tannin, yeast nutrient and yeast and ferment.

BLACK CHERRY WINE

Ingredients:—

2.7 kg black cherries	6lbs. black cherries
250 gm sultanas	½ lb. sultanas
1.5 kg sugar	3½ lbs. sugar
4.5 litres boiling water	1 gall. boiling water
Pectolytic Enzyme	Pectolytic Enzyme
Tannin, yeast nutrient and yeast	Tannin, yeast nutrient and yeast

Method:—

1. Put the cherries into a polythene bucket and pour on the boiling water. When cool add Pectolytic Enzyme and leave 24 hours.

2. Add the chopped raisins and sugar and stir the sugar away. Take a hydrometer reading.

3. Put in the tannin, yeast nutrient and yeast and ferment. Leave for 10 days and strain.

BLACKCURRANT WINE

Ingredients:—

1.3 kg blackcurrants	3 lbs. blackcurrants
1.7 kg sugar	4 lbs. sugar
4.5 litres boiling water	1 gall. boiling water
Pectolytic Enzyme	Pectolytic Enzyme
Tannin, yeast nutrient and yeast	Tannin, yeast nutrient and yeast

Method:—

1. Pick the blackcurrants from the stalks into a plastic bucket. Pour on the boiling water.
2. Leave to cool and then add the Pectolytic Enzyme.
3. Squeeze and stir daily for 7-10 days and then strain.
4. Stir in the sugar and take a hydrometer reading.
5. Add tannin, yeast nutrient and yeast and ferment.

BLAEBERRY (BILBERRY OR WHORTLEBERRY) WINE

Ingredients:—

2.7 kg blaeberries	6 lbs. blaeberries
1.5 kg sugar	3½ lbs. sugar
4.5 litres cold water	1 gall. cold water
2 Campden tablets	2 Campden tablets
Tannin, yeast nutrient and yeast	Tannin, yeast nutrient and yeast

Method:—

1. Put the blaeberries into the cold water adding the crushed Campden tablets. Stir and mash for 6 days, then strain.
2. Into the liquid put the sugar and stir until it is dissolved. Take a reading with the hydrometer.
3. Add tannin, yeast nutrient and yeast and ferment.

BRAMBLE CLARET

Ingredients:—

2.7 kg brambles (blackberries)	6 lbs. brambles (blackberries)
0.5 kg sloes	1 lb. sloes
1.5 kg sugar	3½ lbs. sugar
4.5 litres boiling water	1 gall. boiling water
Pectolytic Enzyme	Pectolytic Enzyme
Tannin, yeast nutrient and yeast	Tannin, yeast nutrient and yeast

Method:—

1. Pour the boiling water over the brambles. When cool add the Pectolytic Enzyme.

2. Stir and squeeze daily for 6 days, then strain.

3. To the liquor add sloes and sugar. Stir away the sugar and mash up the sloes. Take a reading with the hydrometer.

4. Add tannin, yeast nutrient and yeast and ferment.

BRAMBLE LIQUEUR (1)
(Swarland)

Ingredients:—

4 kg brambles	9 lbs. brambles
2.7 kg sugar	6 lbs. sugar
4.5 litres boiling water	1 gall boiling water
Pectolytic Enzyme	Pectolytic Enzyme
Tannin, yeast nutrient and yeast	Tannin, yeast nutrient and yeast

Method:—

1. Boil the water and pour it over the fruit. When cool add the Pectolytic Enzyme. Let it stand 7 days, squeezing and stirring daily.

2. Strain and squeeze every drop of liquid from the fruit through a nylon sieve. Then put it through a fine nylon bag.

3. Add the sugar and take a reading with the hydrometer.

4. Put in the tannin, yeast nutrient and yeast and ferment.

5. When bottled add a little rum or brandy if liked. It makes a fine toddy cure for a cold.

BRAMBLE LIQUEUR (2)

Ingredients:—

An undefined quantity of brambles
from which the juice is extracted.
To every litre (1¾ pints) of pure
juice:—

0.4 kg sugar	14 ozs. sugar
7 gm root ginger (bruised)	¼ oz. root ginger (bruised)
2 teaspoonsful of gin	2 teaspoonsful of gin
Tannin, yeast nutrient and yeast	Tannin, yeast nutrient and yeast

Method:—

1. Put the brambles in a large jar or basin and set it in a pan of boiling water over heat to draw the juice. Measure the pure juice and add the sugar. Stir until it is dissolved.

2. Add tannin, yeast nutrient and yeast and ferment.

3. Add the bruised ginger during the maturing stage, and the gin as it is finally bottled.

BRAMBLE PORT (1)

Ingredients:—

2.7 kg brambles (blackberries)	6 lbs. brambles (blackberries)
0.5 kg sloes	1 lb. sloes
0.5 kg damsons	1 lb. damsons
1.7 kg sugar	4 lbs. sugar
4.5 litres boiling water	1 gall. boiling water
Pectolytic Enzyme	Pectolytic Enzyme
Tannin, yeast nutrient and yeast	Tannin, yeast nutrient and yeast

Method:—

1. Pour the boiling water over the brambles, damsons and sloes. Leave 8 days, mashing each day. Add Pectolytic Enzyme as soon as cool.

2. Strain and squeeze every drop of moisture from the fruit before throwing it away.

3. Stir in the sugar and take a hydrometer reading.

4. Add tannin, yeast nutrient and yeast and ferment.

BRAMBLE PORT (2)
(Jean's)

Ingredients:—

2.7 kg brambles	6 lbs. brambles
1.5 kg sugar	3½ lbs. sugar
4.5 litres boiling water	1 gall. boiling water
Pectolytic Enzyme	Pectolytic Enzyme
Tannin, yeast nutrient and yeast	Tannin, yeast nutrient and yeast
1 glass of rum	1 glass of rum

Method:—

1. Put the brambles in a pan, cover with the water and bring to the boil. Simmer for 10 minutes.

2. Strain and when cool add the Pectolytic Enzyme. Leave 24 hours. Add the sugar and stir it away before taking a hydrometer reading.

3. Put in the tannin, yeast nutrient and yeast and ferment.

4. Add the rum to the bulk just before bottling.

Point to remember: It is quite nice without rum.

BRAMBLE WINE (1)
(Heavy Body)

Ingredients:—

2.7 kg brambles	6 lbs. brambles
0.5 kg wheat	1 lb. wheat
1.5 kg sugar	3½ lbs. sugar
4.5 litres water	1 gall. water
Pectolytic Enzyme	Pectolytic Enzyme
Tannin, yeast nutrient and yeast	Tannin, yeast nutrient and yeast

Method:—

1. Boil the brambles gently in the water for 10 minutes. Then strain, squeezing out all the liquid. When cool add the Pectolytic Enzyme and leave for 24 hours.

2. Add the sugar and the wheat and stir until the sugar has all dissolved. Take a hydrometer reading.

3. Put in the tannin, yeast nutrient and the yeast and ferment.

BRAMBLE WINE (2)
(Gingered)

Ingredients:—

2.7 kg brambles	6 lbs. brambles
14 gm tartaric acid	½ oz. tartaric acid
14 gm ginger essence	½ oz. ginger essence
1.5 kg sugar	3½ lbs. sugar
4.5 litres boiling water	1 gall. boiling water
Pectolytic Enzyme	Pectolytic Enzyme
Tannin, yeast nutrient and yeast	Tannin, yeast nutrient and yeast

Method:—

1. Pour the brambles into the boiling water and boil gently for 10 minutes or so. Then strain and squeeze all the moisture from the fruit before throwing away the pulp. Add the Pectolytic Enzyme and leave for 24 hours.

2. Add the sugar and tartaric acid and stir until dissolved. Take a reading with the hydrometer.

3. Put in the tannin, yeast nutrient and yeast and ferment.

4. Add the ginger to the bulk just before bottling.

BREAD CHAMPAGNE

Ingredients:—

1 kg brown bread	2 lbs. brown bread
1 kg sugar	2 lbs. sugar
4.5 litres water	1 gall. water
2 teaspoonsful citric acid	2 teaspoonsful citric acid
Tannin, yeast nutrient and yeast	Tannin, yeast nutrient and yeast

Method:—

1. Cut the bread into slices and toast it — but on no account burn it or get it too dark brown.

2. Cover the bread with the water in which the sugar has been dissolved. Take a reading with the hydrometer.

3. Add the citric acid, tannin, yeast nutrient and the yeast and ferment.

BULLACE PORT (1)

Ingredients:—

2.7 kg bullace plums (black ripe)	6 lbs. bullace plums (black ripe)
1.5 kg sugar	3½ lbs. sugar
4.5 litres boiling water	1 gall. boiling water
Pectolytic Enzyme	Pectolytic Enzyme
Tannin, yeast nutrient and yeast	Tannin, yeast nutrient and yeast

Method:—

1. Cover the plums with boiling water. When cool add the Pectolytic Enzyme. Stir and squeeze the fruit every day for 7-10 days.
2. Strain and then stir in the sugar until dissolved. Take a hydrometer reading.
3. Add the tannin, yeast nutrient and yeast and ferment.

(This is a fruit growing wild in some parts of Yorkshire. I have seen it at Cropton and Newton-under-Roseberry and it is a cross between a plum and a sloe.)

BULLACE PORT (2)
(Extra Heavy)

Ingredients:—

2.7 kg bullace plums	6 lbs. bullace plums
0.5 kg wheat	1 lb. wheat
125 gm large raisins	¼ lb. large raisins
1.7 kg sugar	4 lbs. sugar
4.5 litres boiling water	1 gall. boiling water
Pectolytic Enzyme	Pectolytic Enzyme
Tannin, yeast nutrient and yeast	Tannin, yeast nutrient and yeast

Method:—

1. Put the plums in a bucket, add the boiling water and leave to cool. Stir and smash up the fruit and add the Pectolytic Enzyme. Now stir round every day for 3 days.
2. Add the sugar, wheat and the chopped raisins and stir until the sugar has all dissolved. Take a hydrometer reading.
3. Put in the tannin, yeast nutrient and yeast and ferment. After one week strain and then continue the fermentation.

BURNET PORT (1)

In Westmorland and Durham they make a port-like wine from Burnet, a herb which grows on a slender stalk with a purple plume like a seed pod.

Ingredients:—

3.4 litres burnet heads	3 qts. burnet heads
1.3 kg sugar	3 lbs. sugar
4.5 litres boiling water	1 gall. boiling water
2 teaspoonsful citric acid	2 teaspoonsful citric acid
Tannin, yeast nutrient and yeast	Tannin, yeast nutrient and yeast

Method:—

1. Pour the boiling water over the burnets. Stand 3 nights, then strain and throw away the pulp.
2. Add the sugar to the liquid and boil gently for 30 minutes.
3. Stand until cool then take a reading with the hydrometer.
4. Stir in the citric acid and add the tannin, yeast nutrient and the yeast and ferment.

BURNET PORT (2)

Ingredients:—

3.4 litres burnet heads	3 qts. burnet heads
1.7 kg sugar	4 lbs. sugar
4.5 litres boiling water	1 gall. boiling water
2 oranges and 2 lemons	2 oranges and 2 lemons
Tannin, yeast nutrient and yeast	Tannin, yeast nutrient and yeast

Method:—

1. Pour the boiling water over the burnets. Put a cover over the bucket and let them stand for 24 hours and then strain.
2. Add the juice and thinly pared rinds of the oranges and lemons and the sugar. Stir the latter away and take a reading with the hydrometer.
3. Put in the tannin, yeast nutrient and the yeast and ferment.

CARNATION WINE

Ingredients:—

2 litres "Pinks" (white)	3½ pints "Pinks" (white)
250 gm raisins	½ lb. raisins
1.3 kg sugar	3 lbs. sugar
4.5 litres boiling water	1 gall. boiling water
2 oranges and 2 lemons	2 oranges and 2 lemons
Tannin, yeast nutrient and yeast	Tannin, yeast nutrient and yeast.

Method:—

1. Put the flower heads into a bucket. Pour the boiling water over and leave for 3 days, stirring daily, then squeeze out the flowers.

2. Add the juice and thinly pared rinds of the fruit, the raisins and the sugar. Stir the latter away and take a hydrometer reading.

3. Add the tannin, yeast nutrient and the yeast and ferment.

CARROT WINE

Ingredients:—

2.7 kg carrots	6 lbs. carrots
1.5 kg sugar	3½ lbs. sugar
4.5 litres water	1 gall. water
2 oranges and 2 lemons	2 oranges and 2 lemons
Pectolytic Enzyme	Pectolytic Enzyme
Tannin, yeast nutrient and yeast	Tannin, yeast nutrient and yeast

Method:—

1. Wash the carrots well but do not peel. Put into the water and bring to the boil then simmer very gently until the carrots are very tender. Use the carrots for food and strain the liquid. Add Pectolytic Enzyme and leave for 24 hours.

2. Add the juice and thinly pared rinds of the oranges and lemons and the sugar. Stir well and then take a reading with the hydrometer.

3. Put in the tannin, yeast nutrient and yeast and ferment.

CELERY WINE

Ingredients:—

1.7 kg celery (green and white)	4 lbs. celery (green and white)
1.3 kg Demerara sugar	3 lbs. Demerara sugar
4.5 litres water	1 gall. water
2 teaspoonsful citric acid	2 teaspoonsful citric acid
Pectolytic Enzyme	Pectolytic Enzyme
Tannin, yeast nutrient and yeast	Tannin, yeast nutrient and yeast

Method:—

1. Cut the celery into short lengths and boil until tender. Strain the celery out and use the celery for food as a vegetable with white sauce.

2. Stir in the sugar and when cool add the Pectolytic Enzyme. Leave for 24 hours.

3. Add citric acid and take a hydrometer reading. Put in the tannin, yeast nutrient and yeast and ferment.

CHAMPAGNE

Ingredients:—

0.7 kg cracked maize (Indian Corn)	1½ lbs. cracked maize (Indian Corn)
0.5 kg large raisins	1 lb. large raisins
2 kg sugar	4½ lbs. sugar
4.5 litres water	1 gall. water
4 oranges and 2 lemons	4 oranges and 2 lemons
2 Campden tablets	2 Campden tablets
Tannin, yeast nutrient and yeast	Tannin, yeast nutrient and yeast

Method:—

1. Put the maize, sugar, chopped raisins, fruit juices and the thinly pared rinds into a plastic bucket. Pour on the cold water and add the crushed Campden tablets. Cover over.

2. Steep for 10 days, stirring daily. Strain and take a reading with the hydrometer.

3. Add tannin, yeast nutrient and yeast and ferment.

CHRISTMAS WINE
(Whisky-like)

Ingredients:—

4 potatoes (as big as the closed fist of a small lady's hand)
1 kg large raisins
0.5 kg wheat
1.7 kg brown sugar
4.5 litres hot (not boiling) water
2 teaspoonsful citric acid
Pectolytic Enzyme
Tannin, yeast nutrient and yeast

4 potatoes (as big as the closed fist of a small lady's hand)
2 lbs. large raisins
1 lb. wheat
4 lbs. brown sugar
1 gall. hot (not boiling) water
2 teaspoonsful citric acid
Pectolytic Enzyme
Tannin, yeast nutrient and yeast

Method:—

1. Scrub but do not peel the potatoes. Grate them into a plastic bucket. Add the sugar, wheat and raisins pulled apart. Cover with the hot water.
2. When cool add the Pectolytic Enzyme and leave for 24 hours.
3. Stir in the sugar and the citric acid and take a reading with the hydrometer.
4. Add the tannin, yeast nutrient and yeast and ferment.

CHERRY PORT (1)

Ingredients:—

2.7 kg black cherries
1 kg prunes
1.7 kg sugar
4.5 litres water
Pectolytic Enzyme
Tannin, yeast nutrient and yeast

6 lbs. black cherries
2 lbs. prunes
4 lbs. sugar
1 gall. water
Pectolytic Enzyme
Tannin, yeast nutrient and yeast

Method:—

1. Boil the prunes in the water until very tender, then strain them out and use for food.
2. Put the cherries in a bucket and pour over the hot prune water. When cool add the Pectolytic Enzyme. Stir and press the fruit daily for 7-10 days. Strain.
3. Stir in the sugar and take a hydrometer reading.
4. Add tannin, yeast nutrient and yeast and ferment.

CHERRY PORT (2)
(Very Heavy Body)

Ingredients:—

4.5 kg black cherries	10 lbs. black cherries
0.5 kg wheat	1 lb. wheat
1.7 kg Demerara sugar	4 lbs. Demerara sugar
4.5 litres boiling water	1 gall. boiling water
Pectolytic Enzyme	Pectolytic Enzyme
Tannin, yeast nutrient and yeast	Tannin, yeast nutrient and yeast

Method:—

1. Put the cherries into a bucket and pour on the boiling water. Squeeze and press the fruit daily for 10 days. On the second day stir in the Pectolytic Enzyme. Strain out all the liquid on to the cracked wheat.

2. Add the sugar and stir until it has all dissolved, and then take a hydrometer reading.

3. Put in the tannin, yeast nutrient and yeast and ferment.

CHERRY-RHUBARB WINE (1)

Ingredients:—

2.7 kg rhubarb (use the red rhubarb and leave on all the skin)	6 lbs. rhubarb (use the red rhubarb and leave on all the skin)
1.3 kg cherries (fresh)	3 lbs. cherries (fresh)
0.5 kg raisins	1 lb. raisins
250 gm wheat	½ lb. wheat
1.7 kg sugar	4 lbs. sugar
4.5 litres water	1 gall. water
2 Campden tablets	2 Campden tablets
Tannin, yeast nutrient and yeast	Tannin, yeast nutrient and yeast

Method:—

1. Cut the rhubarb and pour over the cold water. Put in the crush Campden tablets. Leave for 10 days stirring daily. Strain, squeezing out as much of the liquid as possible.

2. Add the sugar, cherries, raisins and wheat. Stir well and take a reading with the hydrometer.

3. Put in the tannin, yeast nutrient and yeast and ferment. Strain after 10 days and then continue the fermentation.

CHERRY-RHUBARB (2)
(Seaham)

Ingredients:—

2.7 kg cherry-rhubarb	6 lbs. cherry-rhubarb
0.5 kg large raisins	1 lb. large raisins
1.3 kg sugar	3 lbs. sugar
4.5 litres boiling water	1 gall. boiling water
Pectolytic Enzyme	Pectolytic Enzyme
Tannin, yeast nutrient and yeast	Tannin, yeast nutrient and yeast

Method:—

1. Cut up the rhubarb very small and cover with the boiling water. Allow to cool and then add the Pectolytic Enzyme. Stir and squeeze every day for 10 days and then strain on to the chopped raisins and sugar.
2. Stir away the sugar and take a hydrometer reading.
3. Add tannin, yeast nutrient and yeast and ferment.

CIDER WINE

Ingredients:—

3.5 kg small apples	7¼ lbs. small apples
1.5 kg sugar	3½ lbs. sugar
4.5 litres water	1 gall. water
2 Campden tablets	2 Campden tablets
Tannin, yeast nutrient and yeast	Tannin, yeast nutrient and yeast

Method:—

1. Leave the skin on and cut the apples up. Place in a bucket with the crushed Campden tablets. Pour on the water and steep for 10 days stirring daily.
2. Strain and add the sugar to the liquid. Stir it away and then take a hydrometer reading.
3. Put in the tannin, yeast nutrient and yeast and ferment.

CLARY WINE

Ingredients:—

2 litres clary blossom (purple tops)	3½ pints clary blossom (purple tops)
0.5 kg raisins	1 lb. raisins
1.3 kg sugar	3 lbs. sugar
4.5 litres boiling water	1 gall. boiling water
2 teaspoonsful citric acid	2 teaspoonsful citric acid
Tannin, yeast nutrient and yeast	Tannin, yeast nutrient and yeast

Method:—

1. Dissolve the sugar in the boiling water and then pour it over the clary blossoms.

2. When cool take a reading with the hydrometer and then add the chopped raisins, citric acid, tannin, yeast nutrient and yeast and ferment.

3. After 10 days strain off the liquid and continue the fermentation.

CLOVER WINE

Ingredients:—

4½ litres clover blossoms	1 gall. clover blossoms
30 gm bruised root ginger	1 oz. bruised root ginger
1.3 kg sugar	3 lbs. sugar
4.5 litres water	1 gall. water
2 oranges and 2 lemons	2 oranges and 2 lemons
Tannin, yeast nutrient and yeast	Tannin, yeast nutrient and yeast

Method:—

1. Pick the flowers and let them dry in the sun.

2. Put the flowers, water and sugar into a pan and bring to the boil. Add the bruised ginger and allow to cool.

3. Strain and add the juice and thinly pared rinds of the oranges and lemons. Take a reading with the hydrometer.

4. Put in the tannin, yeast nutrient and the yeast and ferment.

CLOVE WINE

Ingredients:—

30 gm whole cloves	1 oz. whole cloves
30 gm bruised root ginger	1 oz. bruised root ginger
1.3 kg Demerara sugar	3 lbs. Demerara sugar
4.5 litres water	1 gall. water
1 Seville orange	1 Seville orange
3 lemons	3 lemons
Tannin, yeast nutrient and yeast	Tannin, yeast nutrient and yeast

Method:—

1. Thinly peel the yellow rind from the orange and lemons and put in a muslin bag with the ginger and cloves. Put in the water and simmer gently for about one hour.

2. Pour the hot liquid on to the sugar which has been placed in a polythene bucket. Stir to dissolve the sugar and then leave to cool. Take a hydrometer reading.

3. Add the juices from the orange and lemons and then put in the tannin, yeast nutrient and yeast and ferment.

COLTSFOOT WINE (1)

Ingredients:—

3.4 litres coltsfoot flowers	3 qts. coltsfoot flowers
(These must be dried in the sun)	(These must be dried in the sun)
0.6 litre dandelion leaves	1 pint dandelion leaves
250 gm raisins	½ lb. raisins
1.5 kg sugar	3½ lbs. sugar
4.5 litres water	1 gall. water
3 lemons	3 lemons
Tannin, yeast nutrient and yeast	Tannin, yeast nutrient and yeast

Method:—

1. Boil the flowers, leaves and water together for 20 minutes then strain.

2. Pour the liquid into a bucket containing the chopped raisins, sugar and thinly pared rinds of the lemons. Stir until the sugar is dissolved and when quite cool add the lemon juice and take a hydrometer reading.

3. Add tannin, yeast nutrient and yeast and ferment.

COLTSFOOT WINE (2)

Ingredients:—

2 litres coltsfoot flowers	3½ pints coltsfoot flowers
1.3 kg sugar	3 lbs. sugar
4.5 litres water	1 gall. water
2 oranges and 2 lemons	2 oranges and 2 lemons
Tannin, yeast nutrient and yeast	Tannin, yeast nutrient and yeast

Method:—

1. Put the flowers and thinly pared rinds of the oranges and lemons into a bucket.
2. Boil the sugar and water together to dissolve the sugar and pour over the fruit rinds and flowers.
3. When cool add the juices from the oranges and lemons and take a reading with the hydrometer.
4. Add tannin, yeast nutrient and yeast and ferment.

COLTSFOOT WINE (3)
(Foalsfoot in the North)

Ingredients:—

2 litres coltsfoot flowers	3½ pints coltsfoot flowers
0.5 kg raisins	1 lb raisins
1.3 kg sugar	3 lbs. sugar
4.5 litres water	1 gall. water
1 orange and 1 lemon	1 orange and 1 lemon
Tannin, yeast nutrient and yeast	Tannin, yeast nutrient and yeast

Method:—

1. Begin by drying the flowers on a clean tray.
2. Boil the sugar and water together to dissolve the sugar.
3. Put the chopped raisins, flowers and thinly pared rinds of the fruit into a bucket and pour the hot liquid over it.
4. Allow to cool then add the juices of the orange and lemon and take a hydrometer reading.
5. Put in the tannin, yeast nutrient and yeast and ferment.

COWSLIP WINE (1)

Ingredients:—

4.5 litres cowslip heads	1 gall. cowslip heads
1.7 kg sugar	4 lbs. sugar
4.5 litres cold water	1 gall. cold water
2 teaspoonsful citric acid	2 teaspoonsful citric acid
2 Campden tablets	2 Campden tablets
Tannin, yeast nutrient and yeast	Tannin, yeast nutrient and yeast

Method:—

1. Pour the water over the cowslip flowers. Use all the heads but not the fleshy stalks. Add the crushed Campden tablets and steep for 10-14 days so that the water gathers all the fragrance and colour. Then squeeze out the flowers (but if the flowers go bad before that time take them out).

2. Add the citric acid and the sugar and stir until all the sugar has dissolved. Take a hydrometer reading.

3. Put in the tannin, yeast nutrient and the yeast and ferment.

COWSLIP WINE (2)

Ingredients:—

4.5 litres cowslip flowers	1 gall. cowslip flowers
1.7 kg sugar	4 lbs. sugar
4.5 litres water	1 gall. water
1 orange and 1 lemon	1 orange and 1 lemon
1 glass brandy	1 glass brandy
Tannin, yeast nutrient and yeast	Tannin, yeast nutrient and yeast

Method:—

1. Boil the sugar and water together to dissolve the sugar and then pour it over the thinly pared rinds of the fruit.

2. When cool add the fruit juices and cowslips. Take a reading with the hydrometer.

3. Add the tannin, yeast nutrient and yeast and ferment.

4. Put in the brandy to the bulk before bottling.

CRAB APPLE PORT

Ingredients:—

2.7 kg crab apples	6 lbs. crab apples
1.3 kg blackberries	3 lbs. blackberries
0.5 kg raisins	1 lb. raisins
1.5 kg sugar	3½ lb. sugar
4.5 litres boiling water	1 gall. boiling water
Pectolytic Enzyme	Pectolytic Enzyme
Yeast nutrient and yeast	Yeast nutrient and yeast

Method:—

1. Put the crab apples and blackberries into a polythene bucket and pour on the boiling water.

2. Allow to cool and then stir in the Pectolytic Enzyme.

3. Steep for 7-10 days stirring and mashing the fruit daily.

4. Strain the liquid on to the chopped raisins and sugar and stir until the latter has all been dissolved. Take a hydrometer reading.

5. Put in the yeast nutrient and yeast and ferment.

CRAB APPLE WINE (1)

Ingredients:—

2.7 kg crab apples	6 lbs. crab apples
1.3 kg brown sugar	3 lbs. brown sugar
4.5 litres cold water	1 gall. cold water
2 Campden tablets	2 Campden tablets
Yeast nutrient and yeast	Yeast nutrient and yeast

Method:—

1. Cover the crab apples with water and after 2 or 3 days when they are swollen and soft, break them up with the hand to mush.

2. Add the crushed Campden tablets and steep for 10-14 days stirring daily.

3. Strain the liquid on to the sugar and stir until it has all dissolved. Take a hydrometer reading.

4. Put in the yeast nutrient and yeast and ferment.

CRAB APPLE WINE (2)

Ingredients:—

3 kg crab apples	6½ lbs. crab apples
0.5 kg raisins	1 lb. raisins
0.5 kg wheat	1 lb. wheat
1.3 kg sugar	3 lbs. sugar
4.5 litres water (cold)	1 gall. water (cold)
2 Campden tablets	2 Campden tablets
Yeast nutrient and yeast	Yeast nutrient and yeast

Method:—

1. Cover the crab apples with the cold water and add the crushed Campden tablets. After 2 or 3 days when the fruit is well soaked break up with the hand to mush. Continue to steep, stirring daily for 10 days.

2. Strain the liquid on to the chopped raisins, wheat and sugar and stir until the sugar has all dissolved. Take a reading with the hydrometer.

3. Add the yeast nutrient and yeast and ferment.

CRANBERRY WINE (1)

Ingredients:—

2.7 kg cranberries	6 lbs. cranberries
1.7 kg white sugar	4 lbs. white sugar
4.5 litres boiling water	1 gall. boiling water
Pectolytic Enzyme	Pectolytic Enzyme
Tannin, yeast nutrient and yeast	Tannin, yeast nutrient and yeast

Method:—

1. Pour the boiling water over the cranberries and add the sugar. Allow to cool and then put in the Pectolytic Enzyme. Squeeze the fruit and stir every day for 8 days and then strain.

2. Take a reading with the hydrometer and then add the tannin, yeast nutrient and the yeast and ferment.

CRANBERRY WINE (2)

Ingredients:—

3 kg cranberries	6½ lbs. cranberries
1 kg raisins	2 lbs. raisins
1.5 kg white sugar	3½ lbs. white sugar
4.5 litres boiling water	1 gall. boiling water
Pectolytic Enzyme	Pectolytic Enzyme
Tannin, yeast nutrient and yeast	Tannin, yeast nutrient and yeast

Method:—

1. Boil the water and pour it over the cranberries. When cool stir in the Pectolytic Enzyme. Mash them daily with the hand for 6 days then strain.

2. Add the chopped raisins and sugar and stir to dissolve. Take a reading with the hydrometer.

3. Add the tannin, yeast nutrient and yeast and ferment.

CURRANT PORT

Ingredients:—

1.7 kg dried currants	4 lbs. dried currants
0.5 kg wheat	1 lb. wheat
1.5 kg sugar	3½ lbs. sugar
Pectolytic Enzyme	Pectolytic Enzyme
Tannin, yeast nutrient and yeast	Tannin, yeast nutrient and yeast

Method:—

1. Boil the currants in the water for 30 minutes, then stand to cool. Add the Pectolytic Enzyme and leave for 24 hours.

2. Put in the sugar and stir until it has all dissolved. Take a reading with the hydrometer.

3. Add the wheat, tannin, yeast nutrient and yeast and ferment.

DAISY WINE

Ingredients:—

4.5 litres small field-daisy blossoms	1 gall. small field-daisy blossoms
250 gm raisins	½ lb. raisins
1.3 kg brown sugar	3 lbs. brown sugar
4.5 litres boiling water	1 gall. boiling water
2 oranges and 2 lemons	2 oranges and 2 lemons
Tannin, yeast nutrient and yeast	Tannin, yeast nutrient and yeast

Method:—

1. Put the daisies in a bucket and pour over the boiling water. Stand until next day, then squeeze out the daisies.
2. Add the sugar, chopped raisins, juice and thinly pared rinds of the oranges and lemons and stir until the sugar has dissolved. Take a hydrometer reading.
3. Put in the tannin, yeast nutrient and yeast and ferment.

DAMSON PORT

Ingredients:—

1.7 kg damsons	4 lbs. damsons
1.7 kg sugar	4 lbs. sugar
4.5 litres boiling water	1 gall boiling water
Pectolytic Enzyme	Pectolytic Enzyme
Tannin, yeast nutrient and yeast	Tannin, yeast nutrient and yeast

Method:—

1. Pour the boiling water over the damsons. When cool put in the Pectolytic Enzyme and mash them daily for 7 days to break up the fruit.
2. Strain the liquid on to the sugar and stir until the latter has dissolved. Take a hydrometer reading.
3. Add the tannin, yeast nutrient and the yeast and ferment.

DAMSON WINE

Ingredients:—

1.7 kg damsons	4 lbs. damsons
0.5 kg wheat	1 lb. wheat
1.7 kg sugar	4 lbs. sugar
4.5 litres boiling water	1 gall. boiling water
Pectolytic Enzyme	Pectolytic Enzyme
Tannin, yeast nutrient and yeast	Tannin, yeast nutrient and yeast

Method:—

1. Pour the boiling water over the fruit. When cool put in the Pectolytic Enzyme and mash daily for 7 days to break up the damsons.

2. Strain and add the sugar and wheat to the liquid. Stir away the sugar and take a reading with the hydrometer.

3. Put in the tannin, yeast nutrient and the yeast and ferment.

DANDELION WINE

Ingredients:—

4.5 litres dandelion flower petals	1 gall. dandelion flower petals
1.3 kg sugar	3 lbs. sugar
4.5 litres boiling water	1 gall. boiling water
14 gm bruised root ginger	½ oz. bruised root ginger
1 orange and 1 lemon	1 orange and 1 lemon
Tannin, yeast nutrient and yeast	Tannin, yeast nutrient and yeast

Method:—

1. Wash the dandelion flowers as they are always gritty, then cover them with the boiling water. Let them stand 3 days, stirring often, before squeezing out the flowers.

2. Bring the liquid to the boil and pour it over the thinly pared rinds of the orange and lemon, ginger and sugar. Stir until the sugar dissolves.

3. Allow to cool and add the fruit juices. Take a reading with the hydrometer.

4 Put in the tannin, yeast nutrient and yeast and ferment.

ELDERBERRY GINGER WINE

Ingredients:—

2 kg elderberries	4½ lbs. elderberries
1.5 kg sugar	3½ lbs. sugar
4.5 litres water	1 gall. water
30 gm bruised root ginger	1 oz. bruised root ginger
Pectolytic Enzyme	Pectolytic Enzyme
Tannin, yeast nutrient and yeast	Tannin, yeast nutrient and yeast

Method:—

1. Strip the elderberries off the fleshy stems. Add to the water and boil 15 minutes, then strain, throwing the pulp away.
2. Allow to cool then stir in the Pectolytic Enzyme. Leave 24 hours.
3. Stir in the sugar and take a hydrometer reading.
4. Add tannin, yeast nutrient and yeast and ferment.
5. Add the ginger well bruised when the wine is 6 months old.

ELDERBERRY PORT (1)

Ingredients:—

An undefined quantity of elderberries from which the juice is extracted.	An undefined quantity of elderberries from which the juice is extracted.
To every 4.5 litres of pure juice:—	To every 1 gall. of pure juice:—
1.3 kg sugar	3 lbs. sugar
0.5 kg raisins	1 lb. raisins
Tannin, yeast nutrient and yeast	Tannin, yeast nutrient and yeast

Method:—

1. Take the elderberries as they turn black to get a full red colour. Strip them from the fleshy stalks and put into a large basin or jar.
2. Put the jar in a pan of hot water over heat and draw all the juice from the berries.
3. Strain the juice from the berries and add the chopped raisins and sugar. Stir the sugar away and take a hydrometer reading.
4. Add the tannin, yeast nutrient and yeast and ferment.

ELDERBERRY PORT (2)

Ingredients:—

1.5 kg elderberries	3½ lbs. elderberries
250 gm large raisins	½ lb. raisins
1.3 kg sugar	3 lbs. sugar
4.5 litres water	1 gall. water
1 teaspoonful citric acid	1 teaspoonful citric acid
Pectolytic Enzyme	Pectolytic Enzyme
Tannin, yeast nutrient and yeast	Tannin, yeast nutrient and yeast

Method:—

1. Strip the berries off the fleshy stalks. Put them with the water and boil for 15 minutes when all the goodness will be in the liquor. Strain, throwing away the pulp.

2. Allow to cool then stir in the Pectolytic Enzyme. Leave 24 hours.

3. Pour the liquid on to the chopped raisins and add the citric acid and sugar. Stir until the latter is dissolved and then take a reading with the hydrometer.

4. Add tannin, yeast nutrient and yeast and ferment.

ELDERBERRY PORT (3)
(Strong and rich)

Ingredients:—

3 kg elderberries	6½ lbs. elderberries
0.5 kg wheat	1 lb. wheat
250 gm large raisins	½ lb. large raisins
1.5 kg sugar	3¼ lbs. sugar
4.5 litres water	1 gall. water
1 teaspoonful citric acid	1 teaspoonful citric acid
Pectolytic Enzyme	Pectolytic Enzyme
Tannin, yeast nutrient and yeast	Tannin, yeast nutrient and yeast

Method:—

1. Strip the berries off the fleshy stalks. Boil with the water for 15 minutes, then strain through the coarse and fine strainer.

2. Allow to cool and add the Pectolytic Enzyme. Leave for 24 hours.

3. Pour the liquid over the wheat, chopped raisins, sugar and citric acid. Stir to dissolve the sugar and take a hydrometer reading.

4. Add the tannin, yeast nutrient and yeast and ferment.

ELDERBERRY WINE

Ingredients:—

3 kg elderberries	6½ lbs. elderberries
1.3 kg sugar	3 lbs. sugar
4.5 litres water	1 gall. water
Juice of 1 large lemon	Juice of 1 large lemon
Pectolytic Enzyme	Pectolytic Enzyme
Tannin, yeast nutrient and yeast	Tannin, yeast nutrient and yeast

Method:—

1. Strip the berries from the fleshy stems. Add the water and boil together for 15 minutes.

2. Strain and throw away the pulp and when cool put in the Pectolytic Enzyme. Leave for 24 hours.

3. Add the lemon juice and sugar and stir to dissolve the latter. Take a hydrometer reading.

4. Put in tannin, yeast nutrient and yeast and ferment.

ELDERFLOWER WINE (1)

Ingredients:—

0.6 litres elderflowers	1 pint elderflowers
250 gm raisins	½ lb. raisins
1.5 kg sugar	3½ lbs. sugar
4.5 litres water	1 gall. water
3 lemons	3 lemons
Tannin, yeast nutrient and yeast	Tannin, yeast nutrient and yeast

Method:—

1. Pick the flowers off the thick main stems and put them in a pan with the water and simmer for 15 minutes.

2. Transfer to a plastic bucket containing the sugar, raisins and the thinly pared rinds of the lemons. Stir until the sugar has dissolved. Allow to cool, put in the lemon juice and take a reading with the hydrometer.

3. Add tannin, yeast nutrient and yeast and ferment.

ELDERFLOWER WINE (2)

Ingredients:—

4.5 litres elder flowers (no fleshy green stems)	1 gall. elder flowers (no fleshy green stems)
1.3 kg3ugar	3 lbs. sugar
4.5 litres water	1 gall. water
3 lemons	3 lemons
Tannin, yeast nutrient and yeast	Tannin, yeast nutrient and yeast

Method:—

1. Boil the water and sugar together for 10 minutes.
2. Put the flowerlets and thinly pared rinds of the lemons into a bucket, then pour on the boiling liquid. Allow to cool before putting in the lemon juice. Take a reading with the hydrometer.
3. Add tannin, yeast nutrient and yeast and ferment.
4. After 10 days strain off the liquid and continue the fermentation.

FIG WINE

Ingredients:—

1.3 kg dried figs	3 lbs. dried figs
250 gm raisins	$\frac{1}{4}$ lb. raisins
1.3 kg apples	3 lbs. apples
1.5 kg sugar	$3\frac{1}{4}$ lbs. sugar
4.5 litres water	1 gall. water
Tannin, yeast nutrient and yeast	Tannin, yeast nutrient and yeast

Method:—

1. Boil the figs in the water until very tender. Remove the figs and use them as food.
2. Chop up the apples and raisins and add to the water with the sugar. When quite cool take a hydrometer reading.
3. Add the tannin, yeast nutrient and the yeast and ferment.
4. Strain after 10 days and continue the fermentation.

FLOWER WINE

Ingredients:—

1 litre dandelion blossoms	1 quart dandelion blossoms
1 litre elder blossoms	1 quart elder blossoms
1 litre cowslip petals (no green)	1 quart cowslip petals (no green)
1.5 kg sugar	3½ lbs. sugar
4.5 litres water	1 gall. water
2 teaspoonsful citric acid	2 teaspoonsful citric acid
Tannin, yeast nutrient and yeast	Tannin, yeast nutrient and yeast

Method:—

1. Wash the dandelions because they are gritty, then put all the flowers into a bucket.

2. Boil the sugar and water together and pour it over the flowers. Leave 3 days then strain.

3. Add citric acid and take a hydrometer reading.

4. Put in tannin, yeast nutrient and yeast and ferment.

GINGER LEMON WINE

Ingredients:—

30 gm bruised root ginger	1 oz. bruised root ginger
125 gm raisins	¼ lb. raisins
1.5 kg sugar	3½ lb. sugar
4.5 litres hot water	1 gall. hot water
4 lemons	4 lemons
Tannin, yeast nutrient and yeast	Tannin, yeast nutrient and yeast

Method:—

1. Put the ginger, thinly pared rinds of the lemons and the chopped raisins into a polythene bucket. Pour on the hot water.

2. Immediately add the sugar and stir it away. When cool take a reading with the hydrometer.

3. Finally put in the lemon juice, tannin, yeast nutrient and yeast and ferment.

GINGER WINE (1)
(Non-Alcoholic)

Ingredients:—

14 gm essence of ginger	½ oz. essence of ginger
14 gm capsicum	½ oz. capsicum
14 gm tartaric acid	½ oz. tartaric acid
14 gm burnt sugar	½ oz. burnt sugar
1.3 kg sugar	3 lbs. sugar
4 litres boiling water	7 pints boiling water

Method:—

1. Take a bottle to the chemist's and he will put in all the ingredients except the tartaric acid, which is a powder, and the white sugar.

2. Put the sugar and tartaric acid in a bucket and pour the boiling water over. Let it stand until cold and then add the other ingredients and bottle.

GINGER WINE (2)
(Non-Alcoholic)

Ingredients:—

7.5 gm cayenne	2 drams cayenne
15 gm essence of ginger	4 drams essence of ginger
30 gm burnt sugar	1 oz. burnt sugar
2 teaspoonsful lemon essence	2 teaspoonsful lemon essence
(Take a bottle to the chemist for the above)	(Take a bottle to the chemist for the above)
22 gm tartaric acid	¾ oz. tartaric acid
1.3 kg sugar	3 lbs. sugar
3.4 litres boiling water	6 pints boiling water

Method:—

1. Put the sugar in a polythene bucket, add the contents of bottle from chemist, and boiling water. Stir until the sugar is dissolved. Allow to cool.

2. Add the tartaric acid to the bulk after dissolving it in a little of the wine. Bottle and keep 14 days.

3. This used in equal quantities with soda water makes a fine sharp teetotal cocktail.

GINGER WINE (3)

Ingredients:—

45 gm bruised root ginger	1½ oz. bruised root ginger
0.5 kg raisins	1 lb. raisins
1.3 kg sugar	3 lbs. sugar
4.5 litres water	1 gall. water
2 oranges and 2 lemons	2 oranges and 2 lemons
Tannin, yeast nutrient and yeast	Tannin, yeast nutrient and yeast

Method:—

1. Put the ginger, the thinly pared rinds of the oranges and lemons, and the sugar into a pan. Simmer 30 minutes and strain. Allow to cool.

2. Add the chopped raisins and the juices from the oranges and lemons. Take a hydrometer reading.

3. Put in tannin, yeast nutrient and yeast and ferment.

GOLDEN DROP GOOSEBERRY WINE
(Garden and Golden Champagne)

Ingredients:—

3 kg golden drops	6½ lbs. golden drops
1 tablespoonful raisins	1 tablespoonful raisins
1.7 kg sugar	4 lbs. sugar
4.5 litres water	1 gall. water
2 Campden tablets	2 Campden tablets
Tannin, yeast nutrient and yeast	Tannin, yeast nutrient and yeast

Method:—

1. Pull the gooseberries when ripe and dry and place in a bucket with the crushed Campden tablets. Cover with water, add the chopped raisins and squeeze and mash every day for 10 days.

2. Squeeze out the pulp and strain through a fine nylon bag.

3. Add the sugar and stir well. Take a reading with the hydrometer.

4. Put in tannin, yeast nutrient and yeast and ferment.

GOLDEN GOOSEBERRY WINE

Ingredients:—

3 kg yellow gooseberries	6½ lbs. yellow gooseberries
0.5 kg wheat	1 lb. wheat
250 gm large raisins	½ lb. large raisins
1.5 kg sugar	3½ lbs. sugar
4.5 litres water	1 gall. water
Pectolytic Enzyme	Pectolytic Enzyme
Tannin, yeast nutrient and yeast	Tannin, yeast nutrient and yeast

Method:—

1. Put the gooseberries, sugar, chopped raisins and wheat into a bucket, cover with warm (not hot) water and stir until the sugar has dissolved. When cool add Pectolytic Enzyme and leave 24 hours.

2. Take a reading with the hydrometer and stir in the tannin, yeast nutrient and yeast. Put to ferment.

3. After 10 days strain and continue the fermentation.

GOLDEN PLUM WINE (1)

Ingredients:—

3 kg yellow plums – very ripe	6½ lbs. yellow plums – very ripe
1.7 kg Demerara sugar	4 lbs. Demerara sugar
4.5 litres cold water	1 gall. cold water
2 Campden tablets	2 Campden tablets
Tannin, yeast nutrient and yeast	Tannin, yeast nutrient and yeast

Method:—

1. Put the plums and water in a bucket together with the crushed Campden tablets. Squeeze and stir daily for 8 days.

2. Strain out the pulp and squeeze every drop of moisture from it before throwing it away.

3. Stir in the sugar until dissolved and take a hydrometer reading.

4. Add tannin, yeast nutrient and yeast and ferment.

GOLDEN PLUM WINE (2)
(Extra strong)

Ingredients:—

3 kg plums	6½ lbs. plums
0.5 kg wheat	1 lb wheat
1.7 kg Demerara sugar	4 lbs. Demerara sugar
4.5 litres water — tepid	1 gall. water — tepid
Tannin, yeast nutrient and yeast	Tannin, yeast nutrient and yeast

Method:—

1. Put the plums, water, wheat and sugar into a bucket and stir until the sugar has all dissolved.
2. When cold take a reading with the hydrometer.
3. Add the tannin, yeast nutrient and yeast and ferment.
4. Strain after 10 days and continue the fermentation.

GOLDEN WINE

Ingredients:—

2 kg yellow gooseberries	4½ lbs. yellow gooseberries
0.7 kg white currants	1½ lbs. white currants
0.5 kg raisins	1 lb. raisins
0.5 kg wheat	1 lb. wheat
1.7 kg sugar	4 lbs. sugar
4.5 litres warm water	1 gall. warm water
Tannin, yeast nutrient and yeast	Tannin, yeast nutrient and yeast

Method:—

1. Put the gooseberries, currants, sugar, chopped raisins and wheat in a bucket. Cover with warm water and stir to dissolve the sugar. Allow to go cold.
2. Take a hydrometer reading and then add the tannin, yeast nutrient and yeast and ferment.

GRAPE PORT

Ingredients:—

3 kg green grapes	6½ lbs. green grapes
1 kg ripe blackberries	2 lbs. ripe blackberries
1.7 kg sugar	4 lbs. sugar
4.5 litres water	1 gall. water
2 Campden tablets	2 Campden tablets
Pectolytic Enzyme	Pectolytic Enzyme
Tannin, yeast nutrient and yeast	Tannin, yeast nutrient and yeast

Method:—

1. Simmer the blackberries in 0.5 litres (1 pint) of the water for 15 minutes. Strain and allow to cool.

2. Put the blackberry juice, the remainder of the water and the grapes into a bucket together with the crushed Campden tablets and Pectolytic Enzyme. Squeeze and stir daily for 10-14 days. Strain.

3. Add the sugar and stir until it is dissolved. Take a reading with the hydrometer.

4. Put in tannin, yeast nutrient and yeast and ferment.

GRAPE WINE (1)

Ingredients:—

2.7 kg grapes (any kind)	6 lbs. grapes (any kind)
1.5 kg white sugar	3½ lbs. white sugar
4.5 litres cold water	1 gall. cold water
2 Campden tablets	2 Campden tablets
Yeast nutrient and yeast	Yeast nutrient and yeast

Method:—

1. Bruise each grape between finger and thumb and cover with the cold water containing the crushed Campden tablets.

2. Stir and press the grapes for 7 days, then strain, throwing away the pulp.

3. Add the sugar and stir until dissolved. Take a hydrometer reading.

4. Put in yeast nutrient and yeast and ferment.

GRAPE WINE (2)

Ingredients:—

1.7 kg grapes (any kind)
12 vine leaves (give a fine, sharp flavour)
1.7 kg sugar
4.5 litres warm water
Tannin, yeast nutrient and yeast

4 lbs. grapes (any kind)
12 vine leaves (give a fine, sharp flavour)
4 lbs. sugar
1 gall. warm water
Tannin, yeast nutrient and yeast

Method:—

1. Put the grapes and vine leaves into a bucket and pour on the warm water. Add the sugar and stir it away.
2. On the second day squeeze all the grapes to burst them and take a reading with the hydrometer.
3. Put in the tannin, yeast nutrient and yeast and ferment.

GRAPE WINE (3)
(Northrop)

Ingredients:—

1.7 kg grapes (unevenly ripened ones in a cold greenhouse was what I used)
4.5 litres boiling water
1.7 kg white sugar
Tannin, yeast nutrient and yeast

4 lbs. grapes (unevenly ripened ones in a cold greenhouse was what I used)
1 gall. boiling water
4 lbs. white sugar
Tannin, yeast nutrient and yeast

Method:—

1. Pour the water over the grapes and steep for 10-14 days, mashing and stirring every day. Strain off the liquid.
2. Stir in the sugar and take a hydrometer reading.
3. Add tannin, yeast nutrient and yeast and ferment.

GRAPE WINE (4)
(Stockton)

Ingredients:—

1.3 kg cheap small black grapes	3 lbs. cheap small black grapes
1.3 kg sugar	3 lbs. sugar
4.5 litres cold water	1 gall. cold water
2 Campden tablets	2 Campden tablets
Yeast nutrient and yeast	Yeast nutrient and yeast

Method:—

1. Put the grapes in a bucket and crush them. Cover with the cold water containing the crushed Campden tablets. Stand 5 days, stirring several times each day, then strain.

2. Add the sugar and stir until it has all dissolved. Take a reading with the hydrometer.

3. Put in the yeast nutrient and the yeast and ferment.

GREENGAGE CHAMPAGNE

Ingredients:—

1.7 kg greengages	4 lbs. greengages
20 vine leaves	20 vine leaves
1.7 kg sugar	4 lbs. sugar
4.5 litres water	1 gall. water
2 Campden tablets	2 Campden tablets
Tannin, yeast nutrient and yeast	Tannin, yeast nutrient and yeast

Method:—

1. Put the greengages and vine leaves in a bucket and cover with the cold water containing the crushed Campden tablets. Take the vine leaves out in 3 days but mash and stir the plums for 8 days, then strain.

2. Stir in the sugar and then take a hydrometer reading.

3. Add tannin, yeast nutrient and yeast and ferment.

GREENGAGE WINE

Ingredients:—

1.7 kg greengages
1.7 kg sugar
4.5 litres water
2 Campden tablets
Tannin, yeast nutrient and yeast

4 lbs. greengages
4 lbs. sugar
1 gall. water
2 Campden tablets
Tannin, yeast nutrient and yeast

Method:—

1. Pour the water over the greengages and add the crushed Campden tablets. Steep for 8 days, mashing and stirring daily and then strain.

2. Stir in the sugar and take a reading with the hydrometer.

3. Add tannin, yeast nutrient and yeast and ferment.

GREEN GOOSEBERRY CHAMPAGNE

Ingredients:—

3 kg green gooseberries
12 grape leaves
1.7 kg sugar (white)
4.5 litres water
2 Campden tablets
Tannin, yeast nutrient and yeast

6½ lbs. green gooseberries
12 grape leaves
4 lbs. sugar (white)
1 gall. water
2 Campden tablets
Tannin, yeast nutrient and yeast

Method:—

1. Pull the gooseberries when they are large and juicy — but remember they must be bone dry. Put the gooseberries into a bucket with the vine leaves and cover with the cold water in which the crushed Campden tablets have been dissolved. Mash the fruit daily for 10-14 days and then strain out all the liquid.

2. Add the sugar and stir it away. Take a hydrometer reading.

3. Put in the tannin, yeast nutrient and yeast and ferment.

GREEN WINE

Ingredients:—

A good big bouquet of balm (stalks and leaves are used)
0.5 kg raisins
1.3 kg sugar
4.5 litres water – boiling
2 teaspoonsful citric acid
Tannin, yeast nutrient and yeast

A good big bouquet of balm (stalks and leaves are used)
1 lb. raisins
3 lbs. sugar
1 gall. water – boiling
2 teaspoonsful citric acid
Tannin, yeast nutrient and yeast

Method:—

1. Pour the boiling water over the balm. Leave 3 days then take out the balm, pressing out all the moisture.

2. Add the sugar and chopped raisins and the citric acid. Take a reading with the hydrometer.

3. Stir in the tannin, yeast nutrient and yeast and ferment.

HEATHER WINE

Ingredients:—

Take a large bunch of heather when in full bloom
1.5 kg sugar
4.5 litres water
2 oranges and 2 lemons
Tannin, yeast nutrient and yeast

Take a large bunch of heather when in full bloom
3½ lbs. sugar
1 gall. water
2 oranges and 2 lemons
Tannin, yeast nutrient and yeast

Method:—

1. Cover the heather with the water and boil for 1 hour. Strain off the liquid and allow to cool.

2. Add the juice and thinly pared rinds from the oranges and lemons and stir in the sugar. Take a hydrometer reading.

3. Put in the tannin, yeast nutrient and the yeast and ferment.

HEDGEROW AMBER

Ingredients:—

3 kg rose hips	6½ lb. rose hips
250 gm raisins	½ lb. raisins
1.5 kg sugar	3½ lb. sugar
4.5 litres cold water	1 gall. cold water
2 Campden tablets	2 Campden tablets
3 oranges and 3 lemons	3 oranges and 3 lemons
Tannin, yeast nutrient and yeast	Tannin, yeast nutrient and yeast

Method:—

1. Pick the hips when they are red and put them into a bucket with the crushed Campden tablets. Pour on the cold water. Steep for 7 days, mashing and stirring every day. Then strain and throw away the pulp.

2. Add the sugar, raisins, juice and thinly pared rinds of the oranges and lemons to the liquid. Stir well and take a reading with the hydrometer.

3. Put in tannin, yeast nutrient and yeast and ferment.

3. Strain after 7 days and continue the fermentation.

HEDGEROW PORT

Ingredients:—

1.3 kg ripe blackberries	3 lbs. ripe blackberries
1 kg ripe bullace plums or damsons	2 lbs. ripe bullace plums or damsons
0.5 kg wheat	1 lb. wheat
250 gm raisins	½ lb. raisins
1.7 kg sugar	4 lbs. sugar
4.5 litres boiling water	1 gall. boiling water
Pectolytic Enzyme	Pectolytic Enzyme
Tannin, yeast nutrient and yeast	Tannin, yeast nutrient and yeast

Method:—

1. Pour the boiling water over the brambles and plums and break up the fruit. When cool put in the Pectolytic Enzyme. Steep for 5 days then strain out all the liquid and throw away the pulp.

2. Add the sugar, wheat and chopped raisins to the liquid, stirring until the sugar has all dissolved. Take a reading with the hydrometer.

3. Put in the tannin, yeast nutrient and yeast and ferment.

HIP WINE

Ingredients:—

3 kg rose hips	6½ lbs. rose hips
1.5 kg sugar	3¼ lbs. sugar
4.5 litres cold water	1 gall. cold water
2 teaspoonsful citric acid	2 teaspoonsful citric acid
2 Campden tablets	2 Campden tablets
Tannin, yeast nutrient and yeast	Tannin, yeast nutrient and yeast

Method:—

1. Pick the hips when they are red and put them into a bucket. Add the cold water and the crushed Campden tablets. Leave them to steep for 7 days mashing them daily with your hand or a wooden spoon. Strain out all the liquid.

2. Add the sugar and the citric acid and stir well. Take a reading with the hydrometer.

3. Put in the tannin, yeast nutrient and yeast and ferment.

HOCK

Ingredients:—

6 potatoes the size of an egg	6 potatoes the size of an egg
0.5 kg large raisins	1 lb. large raisins
1.5 kg Demerara sugar	3¼ lbs. Demerara sugar
4.5 litres boiling water	1 gall. boiling water
3 oranges and 3 lemons	3 oranges and 3 lemons
Tannin, yeast nutrient and yeast	Tannin, yeast nutrient and yeast

Method:—

1. Cut the potatoes up small and put them in a bucket with the chopped raisins, sugar, juice and thinly pared rinds of the oranges and lemons. Pour on the boiling water.

2. Allow to cool and then take a hydrometer reading.

3. Put in tannin, yeast nutrient and yeast and ferment.

HONEY WINE

Ingredients:—

14 gm hops	½ oz. hops
1.5 kg honey	3½ lbs. honey
0.5 kg wheat	1 lb. wheat
250 gm raisins	½ lb. raisins
4.5 litres water	1 gall. water
2 teaspoonsful citric acid	2 teaspoonsful citric acid
Tannin, yeast nutrient and yeast	Tannin, yeast nutrient and yeast

Method:—

1. Boil the hops in water for 20 minutes and then strain and make the liquid up to 4.5 litres (1 gall.).
2. When lukewarm add the wheat, chopped raisins, citric acid and honey. Stir to dissolve then take a hydrometer reading.
3. Stir in tannin, yeast nutrient and yeast and ferment.

HOP WINE

Ingredients:—

30 gm hops	1 oz. hops
30 gm bruised root ginger	1 oz. bruised root ginger
250 gm large raisins	½ lb. large raisins
1.3 kg sugar	3 lbs. sugar
4.5 litres water – boiling	1 gall. water – boiling
1 orange and 1 lemon	1 orange and 1 lemon
Tannin, yeast nutrient and yeast	Tannin, yeast nutrient and yeast

Method:—

1. Pour the boiling water on to the hops, leave over-night then strain.
2. Into the liquid put the juice and thinly pared rinds of the orange and lemon, sugar, bruised ginger and chopped raisins. Stir to dissolve the sugar and then take a reading with the hydrometer.
3. Add tannin, yeast nutrient and yeast and ferment.

KITCHEN WINE

Ingredients:—

3 grape fruits	3 grape fruits
3 lemons	3 lemons
3 oranges	3 oranges
0.5 kg raisins	1 lb. raisins
1.5 kg sugar	3½ lbs. sugar
4.5 litres cold water	1 gall. cold water
Tannin, yeast nutrient and yeast	Tannin, yeast nutrient and yeast

Method:—

1. Place in a bucket the juices and the thinly pared rinds of grape fruits, oranges and lemons, together with the raisins and sugar. Stir well to dissolve the sugar and then take a reading with the hydrometer.

2. Add tannin, yeast nutrient and yeast and ferment.

LEMON WINE

Ingredients:—

12 juicy lemons	12 juicy lemons
0.5 kg raisins	1 lb. raisins
1.7 kg sugar	4 lbs. sugar
4.5 litres boiling water	1 gall. boiling water
Tannin, yeast nutrient and yeast	Tannin, yeast nutrient and yeast

Method:—

1. Put the juice from the lemons and the thinly pared rinds into a bucket together with the chopped raisins and sugar. Pour on the boiling water and stir to dissolve the sugar.

2. Allow to cool then take a reading with the hydrometer.

3. Add tannin, yeast nutrient and yeast and ferment.

LIME WINE (1)

Ingredients:—

0.6 litres lime blossoms	1 pint lime blossoms
250 gm raisins	½ lb. raisins
1.5 kg sugar	3½ lbs. sugar
4.5 litres water	1 gall. water
Tannin, yeast nutrient and yeast	Tannin, yeast nutrient and yeast

Method:—

1. Pull the sweetly scented blossoms from the lime trees when the flower is open full, and dry them in the sun.
2. Put the flowers into a pan with the water and simmer for 15 minutes. Pour into a polythene bucket.
3. Add the sugar and chopped raisins and stir until the sugar has all dissolved. Take a hydrometer reading.
4. Put in the tannin, yeast nutrient and yeast and ferment.

LIME WINE (2)
(Very strong)

Ingredients:—

2.3 litres lime flowers	½ gall. lime flowers
0.5 kg wheat	1 lb. wheat
0.5 kg raisins	1 lb. raisins
1.5 kg sugar	3½ lbs. sugar
4.5 litres water	1 gall. water
2 oranges and 2 lemons	2 oranges and 2 lemons
Tannin, yeast nutrient and yeast	Tannin, yeast nutrient and yeast

Method:—

1. Boil the blossoms in the water for 30 minutes, then strain and leave the liquid to cool to lukewarm.
2. Add the sugar, wheat, chopped raisins and the juice and thinly pared rinds of the oranges and lemons and stir until the sugar has been dissolved. Take a hydrometer reading.
3. Put in the tannin, yeast nutrient and yeast and ferment.

MANGOLD-WURZEL WINE
(Make in March)

Ingredients:—

3 kg mangolds	6½ lbs. mangolds
14 gm hops	½ oz. hops
1.3 kg sugar	3 lbs. sugar
4.5 litres water	1 gall. water
2 teaspoonsful citric acid	2 teaspoonsful citric acid
Pectolytic Enzyme	Pectolytic Enzyme
Tannin, yeast nutrient and yeast	Tannin, yeast nutrient and yeast

Method:—

1. Clean the mangolds by washing well and take off the roughest roots. Cut into dice and boil in the water 1 hour, then strain. Allow to cool.

2. Add Pectolytic Enzyme and leave for 24 hours.

3. Put in the hops and the sugar and stir until the latter is dissolved. Take a reading with the hydrometer.

4. Add citric acid, tannin, yeast nutrient and yeast and ferment.

MARIGOLD WINE (1)

Ingredients:—

1 litre marigold flowers	1¾ pints marigold flowers
0.5 kg wheat	1 lb. wheat
1.5 kg sugar	3½ lbs. sugar
4.5 litres cold water	1 gall. cold water
2 Campden tablets	2 Campden tablets
2 oranges and 2 lemons	2 oranges and 2 lemons
Tannin, yeast nutrient and yeast	Tannin, yeast nutrient and yeast

Method:—

1. Put the water, flowers and crushed Campden tablets into a polythene bucket. Stir daily for 8 days then strain and throw the pulp away.

2. Add the sugar, juice and thinly pared rinds of the oranges and lemons and the wheat. Stir the sugar away and take a reading with the hydrometer.

3. Put in the tannin, yeast nutrient and yeast and ferment.

MARIGOLD WINE (2)

Ingredients:—

1 litre marigold flowers	1¼ pints marigold flowers
0.5 kg raisins	1 lb. raisins
180 gm honey	6 ozs. honey
1 kg sugar	2¼ lbs. sugar
4.5 litres cold water	1 gall. cold water
2 large lemons	2 large lemons
2 Campden tablets	2 Campden tablets
Tannin, yeast nutrient and yeast	Tannin, yeast nutrient and yeast

Method:—

1. Gather the flowers on a dry day, cover with water and add the crushed Campden tablets. Steep for 8 days stirring daily. Then strain and throw the pulp away.

2. Add the juice and thinly pared rinds from the lemons, the sugar, honey and chopped raisins. Stir to dissolve the honey and sugar and take a hydrometer reading.

3. Put in the tannin, yeast nutrient and yeast and ferment.

MARROW WINE

Ingredients:—

2.3 kg marrow (leave the seeds in)	5 lbs. marrow (leave the seeds in)
30 gm bruised root ginger	1 oz. bruised root ginger
1.3 kg sugar	3 lbs. sugar
4.5 litres boiling water	1 gall. boiling water
2 oranges and 2 lemons	2 oranges and 2 lemons
Tannin, yeast nutrient and yeast	Tannin, yeast nutrient and yeast

Method:—

1. Grate the marrow and put it into a polythene bucket with the thinly pared rinds of the oranges and lemons and the root ginger. Pour on the boiling water and stand 7-10 days stirring every day, then strain.

2. Put in the sugar and juices from the fruit. Stir well to dissolve the sugar then take a hydrometer reading.

3. Add the tannin, yeast nutrient and yeast and ferment.

MAYFLOWER WINE (1)
(Hawthorn)

Ingredients:—

2 litres May blossom	3½ pints May blossom
0.5 kg wheat	1 lb. wheat
250 gm raisins	½ lb. raisins
1.3 kg sugar	3 lbs. sugar
4.5 litres water	1 gall. water
2 oranges and 2 lemons	2 oranges and 2 lemons
Tannin, yeast nutrient and yeast	Tannin, yeast nutrient and yeast

Method:—

1. Put the May blossom in a bucket.
2. Boil the sugar and water together and pour over the blossom. Let it stand to cool.
3. Add the wheat, chopped raisins, juice and thinly pared rinds of the oranges and lemons and the sugar. Stir to dissolve the latter and then take a hydrometer reading.
4. Stir in the tannin, yeast nutrient and yeast and ferment.
5. Strain after 10 days and continue the fermentation.

MAYFLOWER WINE (2)
(Double Strength)

Ingredients:—

4.5 litres Hawthorn flowers	1 gall. Hawthorn flowers
30 gm bruised root ginger	1 oz. bruised root ginger
0.5 kg large raisins	1 lb. large raisins
1.3 kg sugar	3 lbs. sugar
4.5 litres water	1 gall. water
2 teaspoonsful citric acid	2 teaspoonsful citric acid
Tannin, yeast nutrient and yeast	Tannin, yeast nutrient and yeast

Method:

1. Put the flowers, ginger, chopped raisins and sugar into a polythene bucket and pour over the water which has been brought almost to the boil. Allow to cool.
2. Take a reading with the hydrometer and then add the citric acid, tannin, yeast nutrient and yeast and ferment.
3. Strain after 10 days and then continue the fermentation.

MULBERRY WINE

Ingredients:—

1.5 kg mulberries	3½ lbs. mulberries
1.5 kg white sugar	3½ lbs. white sugar
4.5 litres water	1 gall. water
Pectolytic Enzyme	Pectolytic Enzyme
2 teaspoonsful citric acid	2 teaspoonsful citric acid
Tannin, yeast nutrient and yeast	Tannin, yeast nutrient and yeast

Method:—

1. Put the mulberries in the water and boil for half an hour, then strain.

2. When cool add the Pectolytic Enzyme and leave for 24 hours.

3. Add sugar and citric acid and stir to dissolve. Take a reading with the hydrometer.

4. Put in tannin, yeast nutrient and yeast and ferment.

OAK LEAF WINE

Ingredients:—

9 litres oak leaves	2 galls. oak leaves
14 gm bruised root ginger	½ oz. bruised root ginger
1.7 kg sugar	4 lbs. sugar
4.5 litres boiling water	1 gall. boiling water
2 teaspoonsful citric acid	2 teaspoonsful citric acid
Tannin, yeast nutrient and yeast	Tannin, yeast nutrient and yeast

Method:—

1. Pick the oak leaves in October when they are withered, put into a bucket and pour the boiling water over. Leave standing 3 or 4 days then strain and throw away the leaves.

2. Add the sugar and ginger to the liquid and boil for 20 minutes.

3. When cool put in the citric acid and take a reading with the hydrometer.

4. Add tannin, yeast nutrient and yeast and ferment.

ORANGE WINE (1)

Ingredients:—

5 Jaffa oranges	5 Jaffa oranges
1 Seville orange	1 Seville orange
1 lemon	1 lemon
0.5 kg wheat	1 lb. wheat
125 gm raisins	$\frac{1}{4}$ lb. raisins
1.3 kg sugar	3 lbs. sugar
4.5 litres water	1 gall. water
Tannin, yeast nutrient and yeast	Tannin, yeast nutrient and yeast

Method:—

1. Put the thinly pared rinds from the fruit into the water and boil for 15 minutes. Strain and allow to cool.
2. Put in the juices from the oranges and lemon, the wheat and chopped raisins and the sugar and stir until the latter has all dissolved. Take a hydrometer reading.
3. Add tannin, yeast nutrient and yeast and ferment.

ORANGE WINE (2)

Ingredients:—

24 oranges (no rind)	24 oranges (no rind)
125 gm large raisins	$\frac{1}{4}$ lb. large raisins
1.5 kg sugar	$3\frac{1}{4}$ lbs. sugar
4.5 litres cold water	1 gall. cold water
2 Campden tablets	2 Campden tablets
Tannin, yeast nutrient and yeast	Tannin, yeast nutrient and yeast

Method:—

1. Peel the oranges but do not use the peel.
2. Cut the fruit into slices and cover with cold water. Add the crushed Campden tablets. Steep for 10 days, stirring daily. Strain and throw away the pulp.
3. Add the sugar and chopped raisins. Stir well and then take a reading with the hydrometer.
4. Put in the tannin, yeast nutrient and the yeast and ferment.

71

ORANGE WINE (3)
(Hovingham)

Ingredients:—

30 oranges	30 oranges
2 lemons	2 lemons
1.5 kg sugar	3½ lbs. sugar
4.5 litres cold water	1 gall. cold water
Tannin, yeast nutrient and yeast	Tannin, yeast nutrient and yeast

Method:—

1. Pare the oranges and lemons thinly and place the rinds in the water to soak. Leave for 4 days, stirring daily, then strain.

2. Squeeze the juice from the fruit and put it into a bucket with the liquid resulting from soaking the rinds. Add the sugar and stir it away before taking a hydrometer reading.

3. Put in the yeast nutrient, tannin and yeast and ferment.

ORANGE WINE (4)
(Spennymoor)

Ingredients:—

12 oranges	12 oranges
0.5 kg raisins	1 lb raisins
1.7 kg loaf sugar	4 lbs. loaf sugar
4.5 litres water	1 gall. water
2 Campden tablets	2 Campden tablets
Tannin, yeast nutrient and yeast	Tannin, yeast nutrient and yeast

Method:—

1. Peel 6 oranges and put the skins in the oven to brown. When well browned pour over them 1 litre (1¾ pints) of boiling water.

2. Cut up the remaining oranges into a bucket and pour over them the remainder of the water (cold). When the brown liquid is cool mix it in also and add the crushed Campden tablets and the chopped raisins. Stir daily for 8 days then strain.

3. Add the sugar and stir until it has dissolved and then take a hydrometer reading.

4. Put in tannin, yeast nutrient and yeast and ferment.

ORCHARD WINE

Ingredients:—

1.7 kg apples	4 lbs. apples
1.7 kg pears	4 lbs. pears
250 gm raisins	½ lb. raisins
1.5 kg sugar	3½ lbs. sugar
4.5 litres cold water	1 gall. cold water
2 Campden tablets	2 Campden tablets
Tannin, yeast nutrient and yeast	Tannin, yeast nutrient and yeast

Method:—

1. Cut up the apples and pears — all the little, unevenly ripened will do — and cover then with the water.

2. Add the crushed Campden tablets and allow to steep for 10-14 days and then strain.

3. Add the sugar and chopped raisins and stir to dissolve the sugar. Take a reading with the hydrometer.

4. Put in the tannin, yeast nutrient and yeast and ferment.

PARSNIP SHERRY

Ingredients:—

1.7 kg parsnips — clean but not peeled	4 lbs. parsnips — clean but not peeled
14 gm hops	½ oz. hops
250 gm malt	½ lb. malt
1.7 kg sugar (Demerara)	4 lbs. sugar (Demerara)
4.5 litres water	1 gall. water
Pectolytic Enzyme	Pectolytic Enzyme
Tannin, yeast nutrient and yeast	Tannin, yeast nutrient and yeast

Method:—

1. Clean the parsnips but do not peel them (weigh after cleaning). Cut into slices and boil gently in half the water until parsnips are tender, then strain.

2. Put the hops in the remaining water and boil until all the goodness is extracted. Strain and add the liquids together. When cold put in the Pectolytic Enzyme and leave 24 hours.

3. Stir in the malt and the sugar until dissolved, then take a reading with the hydrometer.

4. Add tannin, yeast nutrient and yeast and ferment.

PARSNIP WINE

Ingredients:—

1.7 kg parsnips	4 lbs. parsnips
250 gm wheat	½ lb. wheat
250 gm large raisins	½ lb. large raisins
30 gm bruised root ginger	1 oz. bruised root ginger
1.3 kg sugar	3 lbs. sugar
4.5 litres water	1 gall. water
1 large orange	1 large orange
Pectolytic Enzyme	Pectolytic Enzyme
Tannin, yeast nutrient and yeast	Tannin, yeast nutrient and yeast

Method:—

1. Clean the parsnips (weigh after paring), cut them in two and put them into the water and boil gently until they are tender. Strain.

2. Add the sugar and ginger to the liquid and boil for 5 minutes.

3. Allow to cool then put in the Pectolytic Enzyme. Leave 24 hours.

4. Take a reading with the hydrometer, add the juice and rind of the lemon thinly pared and the wheat and chopped raisins.

5. Put in tannin, yeast nutrient and yeast and ferment.

PEA POD WINE

Ingredients:—

2.3 kg pea pods	5 lbs. pea pods
1.7 kg sugar	4 lbs. sugar
4.5 litres water	1 gall. water
2 teaspoonsful citric acid	2 teaspoonsful citric acid
Pectolytic Enzyme	Pectolytic Enzyme
Tannin, yeast nutrient and yeast	Tannin, yeast nutrient and yeast

Method:—

1. Boil the pods in the water until tender and they have turned yellow, then strain. Allow to cool.

2. Add the Pectolytic Enzyme and leave for 24 hours.

3. Stir in the sugar and then take a hydrometer reading.

4. Add citric acid, tannin, yeast nutrient and yeast and ferment.

PEAR WINE

Ingredients:—

1.7 kg pears	4 lbs. pears
0.5 kg raisins	1 lb. raisins
1 cake of shredded wheat	1 cake of shredded wheat
1.5 kg sugar	3½ lbs. sugar
4.5 litres cold water	1 gall. cold water
2 Campden tablets	2 Campden tablets
Tannin, yeast nutrient and yeast.	Tannin, yeast nutrient and yeast.

Method:—

1. Cut up the pears and cover them with the water. Add the crushed Campden tablets, the chopped raisins and the shredded wheat, broken up. Leave 14 days, stirring and breaking up the fruit and raisins every day, then strain.

2. Stir in the sugar and take a reading with the hydrometer.

3. Add tannin, yeast nutrient and yeast and ferment.

A PORT-LIKE BREW
(To make 9 litres or 2 galls)

Ingredients:—

3 kg Rhubarb — cut up small	6½ lbs. Rhubarb — cut up small
3 kg brambles	6½ lbs. brambles
3 kg sugar	6½ lbs. sugar
9 litres water	2 galls. water
2 Campden tablets	2 Campden tablets
Tannin, yeast nutrient and yeast	Tannin, yeast nutrient and yeast

Method:—

1. Cut the rhubarb small and cover with 4.5 litres (1 gall.) of cold water. Add the crushed Campden tablets. Stir daily for 14 days, then strain.

2. Add half the sugar and stir until dissolved.

3. Put in tannin, yeast nutrient and yeast and ferment.

4. A month later, or when the brambles are ripe, cover them with 4.5 litres (1 gall.) of boiling water. Let it stand 8 days, then strain and stir in the other half of the sugar.

5. Add tannin, yeast nutrient and yeast and ferment.

6. After a further month mix the two brews together and allow them to mature as one wine. Simply gorgeous.

POTATO WINE (1)

Ingredients:—

0.5 kg potatoes	1 lb. potatoes
0.5 kg wheat	1 lb. wheat
0.5 kg raisins	1 lb. raisins
1.7 kg sugar	4 lbs. sugar
4.5 litres water	1 gall. water
2 oranges and 2 lemons	2 oranges and 2 lemons
Tannin, yeast nutrient and yeast	Tannin, yeast nutrient and yeast

Method:—

1. Put the wheat, chopped raisins and potatoes in a bucket containing the cold water (peel the potatoes and cut them up very small). Add sugar and stir until dissolved. Take a hydrometer reading.

2. Put in the juice and thinly pared rinds of the oranges and lemons and then add the tannin, yeast nutrient and yeast and ferment.

POTATO WINE (2)

Ingredients:—

2.3 kg potatoes (do not peel)	5 lbs. potatoes (do not peel)
30 gm bruised root ginger	1 oz. bruised root ginger
1.7 kg Demerara sugar	4 lbs. Demerara sugar
4.5 litres water	1 gall. water
2 oranges and 2 lemons	2 oranges and 2 lemons
Tannin, yeast nutrient and yeast	Tannin, yeast nutrient and yeast

Method:—

1. Put the potatoes with the water, bring to the boil and boil for 10 minutes, then strain out the potatoes.

2. Add to the liquid the thinly pared rinds of the oranges and lemons, add the ginger and boil for a further 15 minutes. Allow to cool and then strain.

3. Add the juices from the fruit and stir in the sugar. Take a hydrometer reading.

4. Put in tannin, yeast nutrient and yeast and ferment.

PRIMROSE WINE (1)

Ingredients:—

4.5 litres primrose petals	1 gall. primrose petals
1.5 kg sugar	3½ lbs. sugar
4.5 litres boiling water	1 gall. boiling water
2 oranges and 2 lemons	2 oranges and 2 lemons
Tannin, yeast nutrient and yeast	Tannin, yeast nutrient and yeast

Method:—

1. Pour the boiling water over the flowers and thinly pared rinds of the fruit. Let it stand 5 days stirring and squeezing the contents every day, then strain.

2. Add the juices from the oranges and lemons and the sugar and stir until the latter has all dissolved. Take a reading with the hydrometer.

3. Put in tannin, yeast nutrient and yeast and ferment.

PRIMROSE WINE (2)

Ingredients:—

2.2 litres primrose petals	2 quarts primrose petals
0.5 kg wheat	1 lb. wheat
0.5 kg raisins	1 lb. raisins
1.3 kg sugar	3 lbs. sugar
4.5 litres cold water	1 gall. cold water
2 oranges and 2 lemons	2 oranges and 2 lemons
2 Campden tablets	2 Campden tablets
Tannin, yeast nutrient and yeast	Tannin, yeast nutrient and yeast

Method:—

1. Put the primroses and the crushed Campden tablets into the water and leave 8 days, then squeeze them out.

2. Put the liquid into a polythene bucket and add the wheat, chopped raisins, juice and thinly pared rinds of the oranges and lemons and the sugar. Stir until the latter has all dissolved and take a hydrometer reading.

3. Add tannin, yeast nutrient and yeast and ferment.

PRUNE CHAMPAGNE

Ingredients:—

1 kg prunes	2¼ lbs. prunes
1,3 kg rhubarb	3 lbs. rhubarb
1.7 kg sugar	4 lbs. sugar
4.5 litres water (cold)	1 gall. water (cold)
2 Campden tablets	2 Campden tablets
Tannin, yeast nutrient and yeast	Tannin, yeast nutrient and yeast

Method:—

1. Put the prunes and rhubarb — the latter cut small — into a bucket with the cold water and the crushed Campden tablets. Let it stand 10 days mashing the fruit and stirring it up every day, then strain.

2. Add the sugar and stir it away before taking a reading with the hydrometer.

3. Put in the tannin, yeast nutrient and yeast and ferment.

PRUNE SHERRY

Ingredients:—

1 kg prunes	2¼ lbs. prunes
250 gm raisins	½ lb. raisins
1.7 kg sugar	4 lbs. sugar
4.5 litres cold water	1 gall. cold water
2 Campden tablets	2 Campden tablets
Tannin, yeast nutrient and yeast	Tannin, yeast nutrient and yeast

Method:—

1. Cover the prunes with the cold water. Put in the crushed Campden tablets. Steep for 14 days, stirring and mashing the fruit every day. Strain and extract all the moisture.

2. Add the sugar and chopped raisins to the liquid and stir to dissolve the sugar. Take a reading with the hydrometer.

3. Put in tannin, yeast nutrient and yeast and ferment.

QUINCE WINE

Ingredients:—

2 dozen quinces	2 dozen quinces
250 gm raisins	½ lb. raisins
1.3 kg sugar	3 lbs. sugar
4.5 litres hot water	1 gall. hot water
2 lemons	2 lemons
Pectolytic Enzyme	Pectolytic Enzyme
Tannin, yeast nutrient and yeast	Tannin, yeast nutrient and yeast

Method:—

1. Wash the quinces and then grate them into a bucket. Pour on the hot water. Allow to cool and put in the Pectolytic Enzyme. Steep for 7 days stirring it round well every day.

2. Strain out all the liquid and add to it the raisins which have been chopped, the juice and thinly pared rinds of the lemons and the sugar. Stir until the latter has all dissolved then take a hydrometer reading.

3. Add tannin, yeast nutrient and yeast and ferment.

RAISIN WINE

Ingredients:—

1 kg large raisins	2¼ lbs. large raisins
0.5 kg wheat	1 lb. wheat
30 gm tea	1 oz. tea
1.5 kg sugar	3½ lbs. sugar
4.5 litres water – boiling	1 gall. water – boiling
4 lemons	4 lemons
Tannin, yeast nutrient and yeast	Tannin, yeast nutrient and yeast

Method:—

1. Tie the tea loosely in a muslin bag and pour over the boiling water and let it mash. Lift the bag out when the liquid is lukewarm.

2. Add the chopped raisins, sugar, wheat and juice and thinly pared rinds from the lemons and stir well in. Take a reading with the hydrometer.

3. Add tannin, yeast nutrient and yeast and ferment.

RED CURRANT WINE

Ingredients:—

3 kg red currants	6½ lbs. red currants
1.7 kg sugar	4 lbs. sugar
4.5 litres boiling water	1 gall. boiling water
Pectolytic Enzyme	Pectolytic Enzyme
Tannin, yeast nutrient and yeast	Tannin, yeast nutrient and yeast

Method:—

1. Pour the boiling water over the currants and when cool add the Pectolytic Enzyme. Let it stand for 4 or 5 days, squeezing and stirring every day, then strain taking care to get all the juice from the pulp before throwing it away.

2. Add the sugar and stir it away. Take a hydrometer reading.

3. Put in the tannin, yeast nutrient and yeast and ferment.

RED MEAD

Ingredients:—

2 kg honey	4½ lbs. honey
1.7 litres red currant juice	3 pints red currant juice
0.5 kg raisins	1 lb. raisins
4.5 litres water	1 gall. water
Tannin, yeast nutrient and yeast	Tannin, yeast nutrient and yeast.

Method:—

1. Boil the honey and water together to dissolve the honey.

2. When cool add the red currant juice and chopped raisins and take a reading with the hydrometer.

3. Put in the tannin, yeast nutrient and yeast and ferment.

RED PORT

Ingredients:—

2 kg red brambles (blackberries)	4½ lbs. red brambles (blackberries)
0.7 kg black ones	1½ lbs. black ones
250 gm wheat	½ lb. wheat
250 gm raisins	½ lb. raisins
1.7 kg sugar	4 lbs. sugar
4.5 litres water	1 gall. water
Pectolytic Enzyme	Pectolytic Enzyme
Tannin, yeast nutrient and yeast	Tannin, yeast nutrient and yeast

Method:—

1. Put the brambles and water into the pan. Bring to the boil and boil gently for 10 minutes or until all the goodness is in the water.

2. Strain and squeeze every drop of moisture from the fruit before throwing it away.

3. Put in the sugar and stir it away. When lukewarm add the Pectolytic Enzyme and leave for 24 hours.

4. Add the wheat and chopped raisins and take a hydrometer reading.

5. Put in tannin, yeast nutrient and yeast and ferment.

RED RASPBERRY WINE

Ingredients:—

3 kg raspberries	6½ lbs. raspberries
1.7 kg sugar	4 lbs. sugar
4.5 litres boiling water	1 gall. boiling water
Pectolytic Enzyme	Pectolytic Enzyme
Tannin, yeast nutrient and yeast	Tannin, yeast nutrient and yeast

Method:—

1. Cover the fruit with the boiling water. Allow to cool then add the Pectolytic Enzyme. Leave for 7 days, stirring and mashing the fruit every day. Then strain, getting all the moisture from the pulp before throwing it away.

2. Add the sugar and stir until it is all dissolved. Take a reading with the hydrometer.

3. Put in the tannin, yeast nutrient and yeast and ferment.

RED WINE

Ingredients:—

3 kg red brambles (blackberries)	6½ lbs. red brambles (blackberries)
0.5 kg wheat	1 lb. wheat
1.7 kg sugar	4 lbs. sugar
4.5 litres water	1 gall. water
Pectolytic Enzyme	Pectolytic Enzyme
Tannin, yeast nutrient and yeast	Tannin, yeast nutrient and yeast

Method:—

1. Boil the brambles in the water until every drop of flavour is extracted from them, then strain.

2. When cool put in the Pectolytic Enzyme and leave for 24 hours.

3. To the liquid add the sugar and stir until it is dissolved. Take a reading with the hydrometer.

4. Add the wheat, tannin, yeast nutrient and yeast and ferment.

RHUBARB AMBER
(Thin)
(Make in June, July or August)

Ingredients:—

3 kg rhubarb	6½ lbs. rhubarb
1 kg ripe brambles	2¼ lbs. ripe brambles
1.7 kg Demerara sugar	4 lbs. Demerara sugar
4.5 litres water	1 gall. water
2 Campden tablets	2 Campden tablets
Tannin, yeast nutrient and yeast	Tannin, yeast nutrient and yeast

Method:—

1. Cut the rhubarb up small, put it into a bucket with the crushed Campden tablets and pour over 4 litres (7 pints) of the water. Leave 14 days, stirring and squeezing each day.

2. On the 15th day strain and squeeze every drop of moisture from the rhubarb before throwing it away.

3. Add the sugar to the liquid and stir it away. Then take a hydrometer reading.

4. Put in tannin, yeast nutrient and yeast and ferment.

5. In September or October when the brambles are ripe, put them into a pan with ½ litre (1 pint) of water, bring to the boil and simmer for 10 minutes. Then strain to obtain every drop of liquid.

6. Add the bramble juice to the bulk of the rhubarb and continue the fermentation and maturing processes.

RHUBARB-BEETROOT PORT

Ingredients:—

1.3 kg rhubarb	3 lbs. rhubarb
1.3 kg beetroot	3 lbs. beetroot
0.5 kg wheat	1 lb. wheat
250 gm sultanas	½ lb. sultanas
30 gm bruised root ginger	1 oz. bruised root ginger
1.5 kg sugar	3½ lbs. sugar
4.5 litres water	1 gall. water
2 Campden tablets	2 Campden tablets
Pectolytic Enzyme	Pectolytic Enzyme
Tannin, yeast nutrient and yeast	Tannin, yeast nutrient and yeast

Method:—

1. Cut the rhubarb up and put 2¼ litres (½ gall.) of water over it. Add the crushed Campden tablets and steep for 10-14 days stirring and mashing daily, then strain.

2. Wash the beetroot and boil it in 2¼ litres (½ gall.) of water then when tender use the beet as food and strain the water into the rhubarb liquid. When quite cold put in the Pectolytic Enzyme and leave for 24 hours.

3. Add the ginger, wheat, chopped sultanas and the sugar and stir until the latter has all dissolved. Take a reading with the hydrometer.

4. Put in tannin, yeast nutrient and yeast and ferment.

RHUBARB-BLACKCURRANT

Ingredients:—

3 kg rhubarb	6½ lbs. rhubarb
1.3 kg ripe blackcurrants	3 lbs. ripe blackcurrants
2 kg sugar	4½ lbs. sugar
4.5 litres water — cold	1 gall. water — cold
2 Campden tablets	2 Campden tablets
Pectolytic Enzyme	Pectolytic Enzyme
Tannin, yeast nutrient and yeast	Tannin, yeast nutrient and yeast

Method:—

1. Cut the rhubarb up small and put 3½ litres (¾ gall.) of water over it. Add the crushed Campden tablets and leave for 10-14 days stirring often. Then strain.

2. Add the sugar and stir it away.

3. Simmer the blackcurrants gently in 1 litre (¼ gall.) of water until all the goodness is extracted. Strain and add this liquid to the rhubarb.

4. When quite cold put in the Pectolytic Enzyme and leave for 24 hours.

5. Take a reading with the hydrometer and then add tannin, yeast nutrient and yeast and ferment.

RHUBARB-CARROT

Ingredients:—

2.7 kg rhubarb	6 lbs. rhubarb
1.7 kg carrots	4 lbs. carrots
1.7 kg brown sugar	4 lbs. brown sugar
4.5 litres water	1 gall. water
Pectolytic Enzyme	Pectolytic Enzyme
Tannin, yeast nutrient and yeast	Tannin, yeast nutrient and yeast

Method:—

1. Boil the carrots in the water until tender and use the carrots for food, then strain the hot liquid.

2. Cut up the rhubarb small and pour the hot liquid over it. Allow to cool and then add the Pectolytic Enzyme. Leave to soak for 7-10 days stirring daily.

3. Then squeeze out all the rhubarb and strain the liquid.

4. Add the sugar and stir it away, then take a reading with the hydrometer.

5. Put in tannin, yeast nutrient and yeast and ferment.

RHUBARB CHAMPAGNE (1)

Ingredients:—

3 kg rhubarb	6¼ lbs. rhubarb
20 vine leaves with stems	20 vine leaves with stems
1.7 kg white sugar	4 lbs. white sugar
4.5 litres cold water	1 gall. cold water
Tannin, yeast nutrient and yeast	Tannin, yeast nutrient and yeast

Method:—

1. Cut up the rhubarb very small and mix the vine leaves with it. Add the sugar and the water; stir until the sugar is dissolved, then take a hydrometer reading.

2. Add the tannin, yeast nutrient and yeast and ferment.

3. Strain after 10 days and continue the fermentation.

RHUBARB CHAMPAGNE (2)

Ingredients:—

3 kg rhubarb	6½ lbs. rhubarb
250 gm raisins	½ lb. raisins
1 tablespoonful cracked maize (This you buy at the poultry shop)	1 tablespoonful cracked maize (This you buy at the poultry shop)
1.7 kg sugar	4 lbs. sugar
4.5 litres cold water	1 gall. cold water
4 lemons	4 lemons
2 Campden tablets	2 Campden tablets
Tannin, yeast nutrient and yeast	Tannin, yeast nutrient and yeast

Method:—

1. Boil the maize for ¼ hour in 1 litre (1 quart) of the water, then strain and add it to the bulk, making 4.5 litres (1 gall.) in all.

2. Cut up the rhubarb and place it in a bucket. Cover with the water and add the crushed Campden tablets. Leave 14 days, then strain, and throw away the pulp.

3. Add the sugar and the chopped raisins and the juice and thinly pared rinds of the lemons. Stir until the sugar is dissolved then take a hydrometer reading.

4. Put in the tannin, yeast nutrient and yeast and ferment.

RHUBARB-COWSLIP

Ingredients:—

2.7 kg rhubarb	6 lbs. rhubarb
0.5 litre cowslip yellow pips	¾ pint cowslip yellow pips
1.7 kg sugar	4 lbs sugar
4.5 litres cold water	1 gall. cold water
2 Campden tablets	2 Campden tablets
Tannin, yeast nutrient and yeast	Tannin, yeast nutrient and yeast

Method:—

1. Put the rhubarb (cut up small) with the yellow flowerettes and the crushed Campden tablets into the water. Stand to mash 10-14 days stirring often. Then strain and throw away the pulp.

2. Add the sugar and stir it away, then take a reading with the hydrometer.

3. Put in the tannin, yeast nutrient and the yeast and ferment.

RHUBARB-DAMSON PORT

Ingredients:—

2.7 kg rhubarb	6 lbs. rhubarb
1 kg damsons	2¼ lbs. damsons
2 kg Demerara sugar	4½ lbs. Demerara sugar
4.5 litres water	1 gall. water
2 Campden tablets	2 Campden tablets
Tannin, yeast nutrient and yeast	Tannin, yeast nutrient and yeast

Method:—

1. Cut up the rhubarb small and cover it with 3½ litres (¾ gall.) of the water. Put in the crushed Campden tablets and leave to steep for 10-14 days, stirring often. Then strain.

2. Add sugar to liquid (stir it away) and take a hydrometer reading.

3. Put in tannin, yeast nutrient and yeast and ferment.

4. Later when damsons are ripe, cover them with 1 litre (¼ gall.) of boiling water, squeeze and stir every day for 7 days. Strain, add juice to the rhubarb wine and keep to mature.

Point to remember:— The two must be well blended together, and to do this it is best to turn all the wine into a polythene bucket and stir together fully 10 minutes before putting it back into the fermentation jar.

RHUBARB-DANDELION

Ingredients:—

1 litre dandelion flower heads	1¾ pints dandelion flower heads
2.7 kg rhubarb	6 lbs. rhubarb
1.7 kg sugar	4 lbs. sugar
4.5 litres boiling water	1 gall. boiling water
2 Campden tablets	2 Campden tablets
Tannin, yeast nutrient and yeast	Tannin, yeast nutrient and yeast

Method:—

1. Wash the dandelion flowers in cold water — they are generally very gritty. Then pour the boiling water over them and leave 24 hours. Squeeze the dandelions out and cut up the rhubarb and put it into the liquid together with the crushed Campden tablets. Leave 14 days stirring often, then strain and throw away the pulp.

2. Stir in the sugar and take a hydrometer reading.

3. Add tannin, yeast nutrient and yeast and ferment.

RHUBARB-FIG WINE

Ingredients:—

2.7 kg rhubarb	6 lbs. rhubarb
0.5 kg dried figs	1 lb. dried figs
250 gm wheat	$\frac{1}{2}$ lb. wheat
1.5 kg sugar	$3\frac{1}{2}$ lbs. sugar
4.5 litres cold water	1 gall. cold water
2 Campden tablets	2 Campden tablets
Tannin, yeast nutrient and yeast	Tannin, yeast nutrient and yeast

Method:—

1. Put the figs into the water and simmer until the figs are swollen and juicy and very tender.

2. Strain the water into a polythene bucket and use the figs as food.

3. Cut up the rhubarb small and place it in the fig liquid when it is cold. Add the wheat and the crushed Campden tablets and stand for 2 weeks, stirring often. Then strain and throw away the pulp.

4. Add the sugar to the liquid and stir it away. Take a reading with the hydrometer.

5. Put in tannin, yeast nutrient and yeast and ferment.

RHUBARB GOLDEN CLARET

Ingredients:—

2.7 kg rhubarb	6 lbs. rhubarb
1.3 kg sloes	3 lbs. sloes
125 gm dark barley sugar	¼ lb. dark barley sugar
1.5 kg sugar	3¼ lbs. sugar
4.5 litres cold water	1 gall. cold water
2 Campden tablets	2 Campden tablets
Tannin, yeast nutrient and yeast	Tannin, yeast nutrient and yeast

Method:—

1. Cut up the rhubarb and cover it with the cold water. Add the crushed Campden tablets and let it stand 14 days, stirring often. Then strain.

2. Add sugar, stir till dissolved and take a hydrometer reading.

3. Put in tannin, yeast nutrient and yeast and ferment.

4. Later when the sloes are ripe, pour out the wine and add the sloes, breaking them up with the hand. Add the barley sugar, replace the wine in the fermentation jar and continue the process.

RHUBARB-LOGANBERRY RED WINE

Ingredients:—

3 kg rhubarb	6¼ lbs. rhubarb
250 gm raisins	¼ lb. raisins
1,3 kg loganberries	3 lbs. loganberries
1.7 kg sugar	4 lbs. sugar
4.5 litres cold water	1 gall. cold water
2 Campden tablets	2 Campden tablets
Tannin, yeast nutrient and yeast	Tannin, yeast nutrient and yeast

Method:—

1. Cut up the rhubarb small and cover it with 3½ litres (¾ gall.) of the water. Put in the crushed Campden tablets and let it stand for 10-14 days, stirring daily. Then strain.

2. Add sugar and chopped raisins and stir away the sugar, then take a hydrometer reading.

3. Put in tannin, yeast nutrient and yeast and ferment.

4. When the loganberries are ripe put them into 1 litre (¼ gall.) of water and simmer until all the goodness is extracted (about 30 minutes). Strain and add to the rhubarb liquid, and allow the fermentation to continue.

Point to remember:— Take the loganberries just when they reach the luscious red stage.

RHUBARB-MANGEL-WURZEL WINE

Ingredients:—

1.7 kg mangel-wurzels	4 lbs. mangel-wurzels
2.7 kg rhubarb	6 lbs. rhubarb
0.5 kg large raisins	1 lb. large raisins
1.5 kg sugar	3½ lbs. sugar
4.5 litres water	1 gall. water
2 Campden tablets	2 Campden tablets
Pectolytic Enzyme	Pectolytic Enzyme
Tannin, yeast nutrient and yeast	Tannin, yeast nutrient and yeast

Method:—

1. Cut the mangolds up after well washing and put in the water and boil for 1 hour, then strain and let it cool.

2, Cut the rhubarb up small and pour the liquid over. Add the crushed Campden tablets and the Pectolytic Enzyme. Leave to stand for 10-14 days, squeezing and stirring daily. Then strain.

3. Put the sugar and chopped raisins in the liquid and stir until the sugar is dissolved. Take a hydrometer reading.

4. Add tannin, yeast nutrient and yeast and ferment.

RHUBARB-ORANGE WINE

Ingredients:—

3 kg rhubarb	6½ lbs. rhubarb
6 Jaffa oranges	6 Jaffa oranges
1.7 kg sugar	4 lbs. sugar
4.5 litres cold water	1 gall. cold water
2 Campden tablets	2 Campden tablets
Tannin, yeast nutrient and yeast	Tannin, yeast nutrient and yeast

Method:—

1. Cut up the rhubarb very small and put it into a bucket with the water, the crushed Campden tablets and the thinly pared rinds of the oranges. Leave 14 days stirring every day and then strain.

2. Add the sugar and the juice from the oranges. Stir until the sugar has dissolved and take a reading with the hydrometer.

3. Put in the tannin, yeast nutrient and yeast and ferment.

RHUBARB-PLUM SHERRY

Ingredients:—

2.5 kg rhubarb	5½ lbs. rhubarb
2.5 kg plums (any sort)	5½ lbs. plums (any sort)
1.7 kg sugar	4 lbs. sugar
4.5 litres boiling water	1 gall. boiling water
2 Campden tablets	2 Campden tablets
Tannin, yeast nutrient and yeast	Tannin, yeast nutrient and yeast

Method:—

1. Cut up the rhubarb. Add the plums, the crushed Campden tablets and the water and let all mash 14 days, stirring and squeezing the fruit daily.

2, Strain the pulp out and add the sugar and stir until it is dissolved. Take a hydrometer reading.

3. Put in the tannin, yeast nutrient and yeast and ferment.

RHUBARB PORT
(Extra good)

Ingredients:—

3 kg rhubarb	6½ lbs. rhubarb
250 gm large raisins	½ lb. large raisins
1.7 kg sugar	4 lbs. sugar
4.5 litres cold water	1 gall. cold water
Bramble juice to make it a rich red	Bramble juice to make it a rich red
6 lemons	6 lemons
2 Campden tablets	2 Campden tablets
Tannin, yeast nutrient and yeast	Tannin, yeast nutrient and yeast

Method:—

1. Cut up the rhubarb small and cover with cold water. Add the lemon juice, chopped raisins and crushed Campden tablets.

2. Let it stand 12 days, stirring every day, then strain and throw away the pulp.

3. Add the sugar and stir it in. Take a reading with the hydrometer.

4. Put in tannin, yeast nutrient and yeast and ferment.

5. Later when the brambles are ripe add sufficient bramble juice to make the wine a deep rich red, then continue the fermentation and maturing processes.

Note:— to extract the bramble juice, put the brambles in a jar and set it in a pan of hot water until the juice flows freely.

RHUBARB RED WINE (1)

Ingredients:—

2.7 kg rhubarb	6 lbs. rhubarb
1 litre raspberry juice	1¼ pints raspberry juice
1.7 kg white sugar	4 lbs. white sugar
4.5 litres water	1 gall. water
2 Campden tablets	2 Campden tablets
Tannin, yeast nutrient and yeast	Tannin, yeast nutrient and yeast

Method:—

1. Cut up the rhubarb small and put it into a bucket with the crushed Campden tablets. Cover with cold water and stir daily for 10-14 days. Strain and squeeze all the moisture from the pulp.

2. Add sugar and stir to dissolve it. Take a hydrometer reading.

3. Put in tannin, yeast nutrient and yeast and ferment.

4. When the raspberries are ripe extract the juice over a little heat and add it to the brew. Then continue the fermenting and maturing processes.

RHUBARB RED WINE (2)

Ingredients:—

1.5 kg rhubarb	3¼ lbs. rhubarb
1.5 kg very ripe red gooseberries	3¼ lbs. very ripe red gooseberries
1.7 kg sugar	4 lbs. sugar
4.5 litres cold water	1 gall. cold water
Pectolytic Enzyme	Pectolytic Enzyme
2 Campden tablets	2 Campden tablets
Tannin, yeast nutrient and yeast	Tannin, yeast nutrient and yeast

Method:

1. Cut up rhubarb, cover with half of the water and add the crushed Campden tablets. Stir every day for 10-14 days, then strain and squeeze out all the moisture.

2. Bring the remaining cold water to the boil and put into it the gooseberries and gently simmer until the goodness is out of the berries. Strain and throw the pulp away. Unite the two liquids and allow to cool. Put in the Pectolytic Enzyme and leave for 24 hours.

3. Stir in the sugar and then take a hydrometer reading.

4. Add tannin, yeast nutrient and yeast and ferment.

RHUBARB-ROSE WINE

Ingredients:—

2.7 kg rhubarb	6 lbs. rhubarb
2 litres red rose petals	3½ pints red rose petals
1.7 kg sugar	4 lbs. sugar
4.5 litres boiling water	1 gall. boiling water
2 Campden tablets	2 Campden tablets
Tannin, yeast nutrient and yeast	Tannin, yeast nutrient and yeast

Method:—

1. Boil the water and pour it over the rose petals. Leave overnight then strain through a nylon bag. Cut up the rhubarb small and put it in the liquid together with the crushed Campden tablets. Leave for 10-14 days, stirring often. Strain again and throw away the pulp.

2. Stir in the sugar and take a reading with the hydrometer.

3. Put in tannin, yeast nutrient and yeast and ferment.

RHUBARB SHERRY
(Make in August, September or October)

Ingredients:—

2.7 kg rhubarb	6 lbs. rhubarb
6 large raisins	6 large raisins
1.7 kg Demerara sugar	4 lbs. Demerara sugar
4.5 litres cold water	1 gall. cold water
2 Campden tablets	2 Campden tablets
Tannin, yeast nutrient and yeast	Tannin, yeast nutrient and yeast

Method:—

1. Cut up the rhubarb very small, put into a plastic bucket with the crushed Campden tablets and cover with the cold water. Let it stand 10-14 days, stirring and bruising the rhubarb every day. Strain and squeeze out all the moisture.

2. Stir in the sugar and take a hydrometer reading.

3. Add the raisins, tannin, yeast nutrient and yeast and ferment.

RHUBARB-STRAWBERRY WINE

Ingredients:

2.7 kg rhubarb	6 lbs. rhubarb
1.3 kg ripe strawberries	3 lbs. ripe strawberries
1.7 kg sugar	4 lbs. sugar
4.5 litres water	1 gall. water
2 Campden tablets	2 Campden tablets
Tannin, yeast nutrient and yeast	Tannin, yeast nutrient and yeast

Method:—

1. Cut up the rhubarb small, cover with half the water.

2. Bring the strawberries to the boil in the other half of the water and simmer until you have a nice colour, then turn into the rhubarb. Allow to cool then put in the crushed Campden tablets. Leave all to mash for 10-14 days, then strain, throwing away the pulp.

3. Stir in the sugar and take a reading with the hydrometer.

4. Add tannin, yeast nutrient and yeast and ferment.

RHUBARB-TOMATO WINE
(This is a grand tonic)

Ingredients:—

2.7 kg rhubarb	6 lbs. rhubarb
1.7 kg tomatoes	4 lbs. tomatoes
1.7 kg sugar	4 lbs. sugar
4.5 litres cold water	1 gall. cold water
2 Campden tablets	2 Campden tablets
Tannin, yeast nutrient and yeast	Tannin, yeast nutrient and yeast

Method:—

1. Cut up the rhubarb small, cover with cold water and put in the crushed Campden tablets. Add the tomatoes and stand 10-14 days, stirring and squeezing the tomatoes every day.

2. Strain and then stir the sugar into the liquid. Take a hydrometer reading.

3. Add tannin, yeast nutrient and yeast and ferment.

RHUBARB-WALLFLOWER PORT

Ingredients:—

2.7 kg rhubarb	6 lbs. rhubarb
0.6 litre blood red wallflower petals (no green)	1 pint blood red wallflower petals (no green)
1.7 kg sugar	4 lbs. sugar
4.5 litres cold water	1 gall. cold water
2 Campden tablets	2 Campden tablets
Tannin, yeast nutrient and yeast	Tannin, yeast nutrient and yeast

Method:—

1. Cut up the rhubarb small and cover with cold water. Add the crushed Campden tablets and leave to mash 1 week, stirring every day. Then add (pressed down) the wallflower petals. Leave to mash a further 3 days, then strain and throw away all the pulp.

2. Stir in the sugar and take a hydrometer reading.

3. Put in tannin, yeast nutrient and yeast and ferment.

RHUBARB-WALLFLOWER WINE

This recipe is exactly the same as the one above except that yellow flowers are used instead of red.

RHUBARB WINE (1)

Ingredients:—

2.3 kg chopped rhubarb	5 lbs. chopped rhubarb
1 lemon (rind only)	1 lemon (rind only)
1.7 kg sugar	4 lbs. sugar
4.5 litres cold water	1 gall. cold water
2 Campden tablets	2 Campden tablets
Tannin, yeast nutrient and yeast	Tannin, yeast nutrient and yeast

Method:—

1. Cover the rhubarb with water and add the crushed Campden tablets. Allow to stand 5 days, stirring daily, then strain out the pulp and squeeze all the moisture out of it before throwing the pulp away.

2. Add the sugar and the thinly pared rind of the lemon. Stir away the sugar and take a reading with the hydrometer.

3. Put in the tannin, yeast nutrient and the yeast and ferment.

RHUBARB WINE (2)

Ingredients:—

2.3 kg rhubarb	5 lbs. rhubarb
0.5 kg large raisins	1 lb. large raisins
1.7 kg sugar	4 lbs. sugar
4.5 litres cold water	1 gall. cold water
0.3 litres sherry (Optional – the wine is quite good without it.)	½ pint sherry (Optional – the wine is quite good without it.)
2 Campden tablets	2 Campden tablets
Tannin, yeast nutrient and yeast	Tannin, yeast nutrient and yeast

Method:—

1. Cut the rhubarb small and cover with cold water. Add the crushed Campden tablets and leave to stand 10-14 days. Strain.

2. Add the chopped raisins and the sugar and stir until the latter has dissolved. Take a hydrometer reading.

3. Put in the tannin, yeast nutrient and yeast and ferment.

4. Add the sherry to the bulk just before bottling.

RHUBARB WINE (3)

Ingredients:—

2.3 kg rhubarb	5 lbs. rhubarb
Juice of 1½ lemons	Juice of 1½ lemons
1.5 kg sugar	3½ lbs. sugar
4.5 litres cold water	1 gall. cold water
2 Campden tablets	2 Campden tablets
Tannin, yeast nutrient and yeast	Tannin, yeast nutrient and yeast

Method:—

1. Cut up the rhubarb very small and cover with the cold water. Add the crushed Campden tablets and leave for 8 days stirring daily. Then squeeze out all the goodness from the pulp before throwing it away.

2. Stir in the sugar and lemon juice and take a reading with the hydrometer.

3. Put in the tannin, yeast nutrient and yeast and ferment.

RHUBARB WINE (4)
(Double strength)

Ingredients:—

5.5 kg rhubarb	12 lbs. rhubarb
2.3 kg sugar	5 lbs. sugar
4.5 litres cold water	1 gall. cold water
4 Campden tablets	4 Campden tablets
Tannin, yeast nutrient and yeast	Tannin, yeast nutrient and yeast

Method:—

1. Cut up one half of the rhubarb very small, put it into a bucket and add two crushed Campden tablets and the water. Leave 7 days stirring often, then squeeze out of the liquid all the rhubarb pulp.

2. Now add the rest of the rhubarb and two more Campden tablets and leave for another 7 days. Stir often, then squeeze out all the pulp.

3. Add the sugar and stir away. Take a reading with the hydrometer.

4. Put in tannin, yeast nutrient and yeast and ferment.

RICE WINE

Ingredients:—

1.3 kg rice	3 lbs rice
0.5 kg large raisins	1 lb. large raisins
1.3 kg sugar	3 lbs. sugar
4.5 litres warm water	1 gall. warm water
Tannin, yeast nutrient and yeast	Tannin, yeast nutrient and yeast

Method:—

1. Put the rice and sugar into a polythene bucket and pour on the warm water. Add the chopped raisins and stir to dissolve the sugar. Take a reading with the hydrometer, when cold.

2. Add tannin, yeast nutrient and yeast and ferment.

ROWANBERRY WINE (1)

Ingredients:—

1.5 kg ripe rowanberries	3½ lbs. ripe rowanberries
1.5 kg white sugar	3½ lbs. white sugar
4.5 litres boiling water	1 gall. boiling water
2 teaspoonsful citric acid	2 teaspoonsful citric acid
Pectolytic Enzyme	Pectolytic Enzyme
Tannin, yeast nutrient and yeast	Tannin, yeast nutrient and yeast

Method:—

1. Pour the boiling water over the berries. Leave to go cold then add the Pectolytic Enzyme. Stand for 6 days then strain.

2. Add the sugar to the liquid and stir it away. Take a reading with the hydrometer.

3. Put in the citric acid, tannin, yeast nutrient and yeast and ferment.

ROWANBERRY WINE (2)

Ingredients:—

2.7 kg rowanberries	6 lbs. rowanberries
250 gm wheat	½ lb. wheat
30 gm bruised root ginger	1 oz. bruised root ginger
1 tablespoonful raisins	1 tablespoonful raisins
1.7 kg sugar	4 lb. sugar
4.5 litres water	1 gall. water
Pectolytic Enzyme	Pectolytic Enzyme
Tannin, yeast nutrient and yeast	Tannin, yeast nutrient and yeast

Method:—

1. Pour the boiling water over the berries and let them stand 4 days, then strain.

2. Put in the wheat, chopped raisins and sugar and stir until the sugar is dissolved. Take a hydrometer reading.

3. Add the ginger, tannin, yeast nutrient and yeast and ferment.

SAFFRON WINE

Ingredients:—

3 kg rhubarb	6½ lbs. rhubarb
Big pinch of saffron (or if in liquid form 1 tablespoonful)	Big pinch of saffron (or if in liquid form 1 tablespoon)
0.5 kg wheat	1 lb. wheat
250 gm raisins	½ lb. raisins
1.7 kg sugar	4 lbs. sugar
4.5 litres water	1 gall. water
2 Campden tablets	2 Campden tablets
Tannin, yeast nutrient and yeast	Tannin, yeast nutrient and yeast

Method:—

1. Cut up the rhubarb and cover with the water. Add the crushed Campden tablets and stir every day for 10-14 days. Strain.

2. Add the sugar and stir until it is dissolved, then add the saffron, wheat and chopped raisins. Take a reading with the hydrometer.

3. Put in the tannin, yeast nutrient and yeast and ferment.

SAGE WINE

Ingredients:—

0.6 litre young sage leaves (well pressed down)	1 pint young sage leaves (well pressed down)
0.5 kg large raisins	1 lb. large raisins
1.5 kg rhubarb	3½ lbs. rhubarb
1.7 kg sugar	4 lbs. sugar
4.5 litres hot water	1 gall. hot water
Tannin, yeast nutrient and yeast	Tannin, yeast nutrient and yeast

Method:—

1. Cut up the rhubarb small and roughly chop the sage. Put into a bucket with the chopped raisins.

2. Pour over the hot water and stir daily for 7 days, then strain and squeeze all the moisture from the pulp.

3. Stir in the sugar and take a hydrometer reading.

4. Add tannin, yeast nutrient and yeast and ferment.

SLOE WINE

Ingredients:—

1.3 kg sloes (gathered in November)	3 lbs. sloes (gathered in November)
1.7 kg sugar	4 lbs. sugar
4.5 litres boiling water	1 gall. boiling water
Pectolytic Enzyme	Pectolytic Enzyme
Tannin, yeast nutrient and yeast	Tannin, yeast nutrient and yeast

Method:—

1. Put the sloes into a bucket and pour on the boiling water. Allow to cool and stir in the Pectolytic Enzyme. Stand for 7 days stirring daily, then strain.

2. Add the sugar and stir it away. Take a hydrometer reading.

3. Put in the tannin, yeast nutrient and yeast and ferment.

STRAWBERRY WINE (1)

Ingredients:—

3 kg ripe strawberries	6½ lbs. ripe strawberries
125 gm large raisins	¼ lb large raisins
1.5 kg white sugar	3½ lbs. white sugar
4.5 litres water	1 gall. water
Tannin, yeast nutrient and yeast	Tannin, yeast nutrient and yeast

Method:—

1. Hull the strawberries and put them in the preserving pan with the water and simmer gently for 15 minutes.
2. Strain and stir in the sugar. Add the chopped raisins and take a reading with the hydrometer.
3. Put in the tannin, yeast nutrient and yeast and ferment.

STRAWBERRY WINE (2)

Ingredients:—

3 kg ripe strawberries	6¼ lbs ripe strawberries
1 kg red cherries	2¼ lbs. red cherries
0.5 kg wheat	1 lb. wheat
1.7 kg white sugar	4 lbs. white sugar
4.5 litres cold water	1 gall. cold water
2 Campden tablets	2 Campden tablets
Tannin, yeast nutrient and yeast	Tannin, yeast nutrient and yeast

Method:—

1. Stand the fruit and water in a polythene bucket, squeezing the fruit every day. Put the crushed Campden tablets, wheat, and sugar into the bucket. Leave 10-14 days, then strain.
2. Take a reading with the hydrometer.
3. Stir in the tannin, yeast nutrient and yeast and ferment.

SULTANA WINE
(Gingered)

Ingredients:—

1 kg sultanas	2¼ lbs. sultanas
0.5 kg wheat	1 lb. wheat
30 gm bruised root ginger	1 oz. bruised root ginger
1.5 kg sugar	3½ lbs. sugar
4.5 litres warm water	1 gall. warm water
1 lemon	1 lemon
Tannin, yeast nutrient and yeast	Tannin, yeast nutrient and yeast

Method:—

1. Mince the sultanas and put them with the ginger, wheat and juice and thinly pared rind of the lemon into a bucket.

2. Cover with the water and stir in the sugar. When cold take a reading with the hydrometer.

3. Add the tannin, yeast nutrient and yeast and ferment. Strain after 10 days.

SWEETHEART WINE

Ingredients:—

2.7 kg apples	6 lbs. apples
6 large Jaffa oranges	6 large Jaffa oranges
1.7 kg sugar	4 lbs. sugar
4.5 litres water	1 gall. water
2 Campden tablets	2 Campden tablets
Tannin, yeast nutrient and yeast	Tannin, yeast nutrient and yeast.

Method:—

1. Cut up the apples small and put them into a bucket together with the crushed Campden tablets and the juice and thinly pared rinds of the oranges. Pour over the water and leave 4 days.

2. Add the sugar and stir it away. Take a reading with the hydrometer.

3. Put in the tannin, yeast nutrient and yeast and ferment.

4. After 10 days strain and then continue the fermentation.

TOMATO WINE

Ingredients:—

3.6 kg ripe tomatoes	8 lbs. ripe tomatoes
1 tablespoonful salt	1 tablespoonful salt
30 gm bruised root ginger	1 oz. bruised root ginger
1.5 kg sugar	3½ lbs. sugar
4.5 litres water	1 gall. water
Tannin, yeast nutrient and yeast	Tannin, yeast nutrient and yeast

Method:—

1. Boil the sugar and ginger in the water for 20 minutes.
2. Turn it boiling on to the tomatoes and salt. Leave to cool.
3. Take a reading with the hydrometer then add the tannin, yeast nutrient and yeast and ferment. After 10 days strain and continue the fermentation.

This is a fine pick-me-up.

TONIC WINE (1)

Ingredients:—

2.7 kg beetroots	6 lbs. beetroots
1.3 kg Demerara sugar	3 lbs. Demerara sugar
0.3 litres stout	½ pint stout

Method:—

1. Wash the beetroots and cut them into thin slices in a bowl. Sprinkle the sugar over the slices.
2. Leave for 2 days then strain off all the liquid and mix it with the stout. Bottle and cork tightly.
3. Take a tablespoonful three times a day.

TONIC WINE (2)

Ingredients:—

1 glass rum	1 glass rum
Small jar of beef extract	Small jar of beef extract
250 gm Demerara sugar	½ lb. Demerara sugar
0.15 litre black beer	¼ pint black beer
0.6 litre Old Tom (old ale)	1 pint Old Tom (old ale)

Method:—

Mix together and take a wine glass-ful daily.

VANILLA WINE

Ingredients:—

2.7 kg rhubarb	6 lbs. rhubarb
4.5 litres May flowers (Hawthorn)	1 gall. May flowers (Hawthorn)
1.7 kg sugar	4 lbs. sugar
4.5 litres cold water	1 gall. cold water
2 lemons	2 lemons
2 Campden tablets	2 Campden tablets
Tannin, yeast nutrient and yeast	Tannin, yeast nutrient and yeast

Method:—

1. Cut up the rhubarb and place it in a bucket with the blossoms and the two lemons cut into slices and the crushed Campden tablets. Cover with the cold water. Leave to steep for 10-14 days stirring daily.

2. Strain and add the sugar. Stir until it is dissolved and then take a hydrometer reading.

3. Put in the tannin, yeast nutrient and yeast and ferment.

VINE LEAVES WINE

Ingredients:—

2.3 kg vine leaves and stems   5 lbs. vine leaves and stems
1.5 kg sugar   3½ lbs. sugar
4.5 litres boiling water   1 gall. boiling water
2 lemons   2 lemons
Tannin, yeast nutrient and yeast.   Tannin, yeast nutrient and yeast.

Method:—

1. Put the leaves into a polythene bucket and pour over the boiling water. Let it stand 3 days, then squeeze the leaves and stems out of the liquid.

2. Stir in the sugar and juice from the lemons and take a hydrometer reading.

3. Add tannin, yeast nutrient and yeast and ferment.

WALNUT WINE

Ingredients:—

1 large bouquet of walnut leaves   1 large bouquet of walnut leaves
250 gm raisins   ½ lb. raisins
1.3 kg sugar   3 lbs. sugar
4.5 litres water   1 gall. water
2 teaspoonsful of citric acid   2 teaspoonsful citric acid
Tannin, yeast nutrient and yeast   Tannin, yeast nutrient and yeast

Method:—

1. Boil the sugar and water together and pour over the walnut leaves. Stand 24 hours then squeeze out the leaves.

2. Add the chopped raisins and citric acid. Take a reading with the hydrometer.

3. Put in the tannin, yeast nutrient and yeast and ferment.

WHEAT WINE

Ingredients:—

0.5 kg wheat	1 lb. wheat
1 kg sultanas (chopped)	2¼ lbs. sultanas (chopped)
0.5 kg old potatoes (chopped finely)	1 lb. old potatoes (chopped finely)
1.7 kg sugar	4 lbs. sugar
4.5 litres hot water	1 gall. hot water
2 grape-fruits	2 grape-fruits
Tannin, yeast nutrient and yeast	Tannin, yeast nutrient and yeast

Method:—

1. Put the wheat, sultanas, potatoes, sugar and juice and thinly pared rinds of the grape-fruits into a bucket.

2. Pour the hot water over and stir until the sugar is dissolved. Allow to cool and take a hydrometer reading.

3. Put in the tannin, yeast nutrient and yeast and ferment.

4. After 10 days strain and then continue the fermentation.

WHIN WINE

Ingredients:—

2 litres whin blooms	½ gall. whin blooms
0.5 kg raisins	1 lb. raisins
1.3 kg sugar	3 lbs. sugar
4.5 litres hot water	1 gall. hot water
2 Campden tablets	2 Campden tablets
2 teaspoonsful citric acid	2 teaspoonsful citric acid
Tannin, yeast nutrient and yeast	Tannin, yeast nutrient and yeast

Method:—

1. Put blooms, water and sugar in a polythene bucket with the crushed Campden tablets. Leave to steep for 7 days stirring every day. Then strain.

2. Add the chopped raisins and the citric acid and take a hydrometer reading.

3. Put in tannin, yeast nutrient and yeast and ferment.

WHITE CURRANT WINE

Ingredients:—

3 kg white currants	6½ lbs. white currants
0.5 kg raisins	1 lb. raisins
1.5 kg sugar — white	3½ lbs. sugar — white
4.5 litres boiling water	1 gall. boiling water
Pectolytic Enzyme	Pectolytic Enzyme
Tannin, yeast nutrient and yeast	Tannin, yeast nutrient and yeast

Method:—

1. Put the currants into a bucket. (I generally rip them off the strap). Add the chopped raisins, sugar and boiling water. Leave to cool then put in the Pectolytic Enzyme. Stir and mash the fruit every day for 7-10 days.

2. Strain and take a hydrometer reading.

3. Put in the tannin, yeast nutrient and yeast and ferment.

YARROW SHERRY

Ingredients:—

2 litres yarrow flowers	½ gall. yarrow flowers
1 cake of shredded wheat	1 cake of shredded wheat
1.7 kg sugar	4 lbs. sugar
4.5 litres boiling water	1 gall. boiling water
4 lemons	4 lemons
Tannin, yeast nutrient and yeast	Tannin, yeast nutrient and yeast

Method:—

1. Pour the water over the flowers and leave 4 or 5 days, then strain.

2. Boil the sugar in the liquid for 20 minutes, then pour it over the juice and thinly pared rinds of the lemons. Allow to cool and then put in the shredded wheat crumbled up. Take a reading with the hydrometer.

3. Add tannin, yeast nutrient and yeast and ferment.

YARROW WINE

Ingredients:—

3.5 litres yarrow flowers	3 quarts yarrow flowers
1.7 kg sugar	4 lbs. sugar
4.5 litres boiling water	1 gall. boiling water
4 oranges	4 oranges
Tannin, yeast nutrient and yeast	Tannin, yeast nutrient and yeast

Method:—

1. Pour the water over the flowers and leave to soak 4 or 5 days, then strain.

2. Put the liquid into a pan with the sugar and thinly pared rinds of the oranges and simmer 20 minutes.

3. Slice the oranges (no pith) into a polythene bucket and pour on the liquid from the pan. Allow to go cold.

4. Take a reading with the hydrometer and add tannin, yeast nutrient and yeast and ferment.

YELLOW RASPBERRY WINE

Ingredients:—

3 kg yellow raspberries	6½ lbs. yellow raspberries
1.7 kg Demerara sugar	4 lbs. Demerara sugar
4.5 litres warm water	1 gall. warm water
Pectolytic Enzyme	Pectolytic Enzyme
Tannin, yeast nutrient and yeast	Tannin, yeast nutrient and yeast

Method:—

1. Put the fruit into a bucket and pour over the warm water. Add the sugar and stir until dissolved and when cold put in the Pectolytic Enzyme. Stir and mash every day for 7 days.

2. Strain and take a hydrometer reading.

3. Add the tannin, yeast nutrient and the yeast and ferment.

RECIPES FOR BEERS, MINERALS, ETC.

APPLE BEER

Ingredients:—

1.7 kg apples	4 lbs. apples
58 gm bruised root ginger	2 oz. bruised root ginger
1 teaspoonful whole cloves	1 teaspoonful whole cloves
1 teaspoonful cinnamon	1 teaspoonful cinnamon
1.3 kg sugar	3 lbs. sugar
9 litres cold water	2 galls. cold water

Method:—

1. Grate the apples up with a suet grater and put them in a bowl with the cold water. Stir every day for a week then strain.

2. Add the sugar, cloves, cinnamon and ginger (well bruised). Stir well and leave overnight.

3. Then strain and bottle, cork lightly for a week, then it is ready for use and tastes delicious.

BEETROOT COCKTAIL

Ingredients:—

1.7 kg beetroot	4 lbs. beetroot
7 gm hops	¼ oz. hops
250 gm malt	½ lb. malt
1.7 kg sugar	4 lbs. sugar
4.5 litres water	1 gall. water
2 teaspoonsful citric acid	2 teaspoonsful citric acid
Tannin, yeast nutrient and yeast	Tannin, yeast nutrient and yeast

Method:—

1. Divide the water into three parts.
2. Clean and cut up the beetroot and place in one portion of water. Boil gently for 20 minutes then strain the beetroot out.
3. Boil the hops in the second portion of water for 30 minutes then strain the hops out.
4. If the malt is the dry corn type, it must be boiled for 30 minutes in the remaining portion of water. If the liquid jelly-like kind, it only needs stirring away in hot water.
5. Put all the three liquids together and measure it. Make up to 4½ litres (1 gall.)
6. Add the sugar and stir until it is dissolved. When quite cold take a reading with the hydrometer.
7. Add citric acid, tannin, yeast nutrient and yeast and ferment.

This was like whisky, brandy and rum mixed and slightly sweetened.

BLACKCURRANT GIN

Ingredients:—

0.9 litres gin	1½ pints gin
Large heaped breakfastcupful of large, ripe, juicy blackcurrants	Large heaped breakfastcupful of large, ripe, juicy blackcurrants
A scant third of a cup of sugar	A scant third of a cup of sugar

Method:—

1. Pick stalks off blackcurrants and add them with the sugar to the gin.

2. Shake every day until the blackcurrants are but a fine sediment in the bottom of the bottle, then strain.

3. Taste, and add more sugar if needed to suit your taste.

BLACK ROB
(For breaking up a cold)

Ingredients:—

2 litres blackcurrant juice	3½ pints blackcurrant juice
1.3 kg sugar	3 lbs. sugar
14 gm whole cloves	½ oz. whole cloves
14 gm cassia buds	½ oz. cassia buds
14 gm bruised root ginger	½ oz. bruised root ginger

Method:—

1. Extract the juice by heating a vessel containing the very ripe blackcurrants in a pan of boiling water — the heat makes the juice run — and it is easily strained off.

2. Put the juice, sugar, cloves, cassia and ginger into a pan. Bring slowly to the boil, stirring to dissolve the sugar, then boil a full 5 minutes by the clock. Add a glass of brandy and bottle.

3. A measure with boiling water is an excellent cold cure.

BRAMBLE VINEGAR
(Strong and Rich)

Ingredients:—

1.3 kg brambles	3 lbs. brambles
1 litre white wine vinegar	1¾ pints white wine vinegar

Allow 0.5 kg (1 lb.) sugar to 0.6 litres (1 pint) of juice

Method:—

1. Pick over the brambles and cover them with the vinegar. Allow them to stand 8 days, stirring often, then strain through a nylon bag.

2. Measure the juice and add the calculated amount of sugar. Put into a pan, bring to the boil and simmer very gently for 5 minutes, then bottle and cork well.

You must be careful in boiling to time or it will jelly. A measure of this is delightful in cold water as a refreshing drink on a hot summer's day or with hot water as a night cap for a cold.

CARROT WHISKY

Ingredients:—

2.7 kg carrots	6 lbs. carrots
1 tablespoonful raisins	1 tablespoonful raisins
0.5 kg wheat	1 lb. wheat
1.7 kg sugar	4 lbs. sugar
4.5 litres water	1 gall. water
2 oranges and 2 lemons	2 oranges and 2 lemons
Pectolytic Enzyme	Pectolytic Enzyme
Tannin, yeast nutrient and yeast	Tannin, yeast nutrient and yeast

Method:—

1. Wash the carrots well but do not peel. Put into the water then bring to the boil. Simmer gently until the carrots are very tender. Use the carrots for food, and strain the water.

2. Into a bucket put the sugar, the thinly pared rinds of the oranges and lemons and pour over the hot liquid. Stir until the sugar is dissolved and leave to go cold. Then put in the Pectolytic Enzyme and leave for 24 hours.

3. Take a reading with the hydrometer and put in the juice of the fruit, chopped raisins and wheat. Add tannin, yeast nutrient and yeast and ferment.

DAISY WHISKY

Ingredients:—

4.5 litres small field daisy blossoms	1 gall. small field daisy blossoms
0.5 kg wheat	1 lb. wheat
0.5 kg raisins	1 lb. raisins
1.5 kg sugar	3½ lbs. sugar
4.5 litres boiling water	1 gall. boiling water
2 oranges and 2 lemons	2 oranges and 2 lemons
Tannin, yeast nutrient and yeast	Tannin, yeat nutrient and yeast

Method:—

1. Put the daisies in a bucket and cover with the boiling water. Stand until next day then squeeze the daisies out.

2. Add sliced oranges and lemons, chopped raisins, wheat and sugar and stir until the latter is dissolved. Take a reading with the hydrometer.

3.. Put in tannin, yeast nutrient and yeast and ferment.

DAMSON GIN

Ingredients:—

1 kg damsons	2¼ lbs. damsons
1 litre gin	1¾ pints gin
0.5 kg brown sugar candy or lump sugar — or barley sugar will do	1 lb. brown sugar candy or lump sugar — or barley sugar will do

Method:—

1. Prick all the damsons with a needle and crush the candy.

2. Put into a big bottle or jar and add the gin. Shake often for 2 months.

3. Then strain and bottle. The longer it is kept the better.

ELDERFLOWER LEMONADE

Ingredients:—

0.6 litres elder flowers	1 pint elder flowers
1 lemon	1 lemon
2 tablespoonsful white wine vinegar	2 tablespoonsful white wine vinegar
0.7 kg loaf sugar	1½ lbs. loaf sugar
4.5 litres water	1 gall. water

Method:—

1. Put all in a bucket adding the lemon cut in four. Let it infuse for 24 hours, stirring often and squeezing the lemon.

2. Then strain and bottle, tying the corks in securely, and lay the bottles on their sides.

FRUIT SYRUPS

Choice of fruits:—

Raspberry, Strawberry, Bramble, Red, Black and White Currant, Loganberry, Victoria Plum, Blaeberry, Cranberry and Cherry. Take the stones from the plum and cherry.

Method:—

1. Put the fruit in a large jar and stand the jar in a pan of boiling water until all the juice is given off, then strain off the juice and when the fruit has cooled enough to handle, squeeze it through a nylon bag. Add this juice to the rest and strain all of it again. Throw the pulp away.

2. Measure the juice and allow 0.5 kg (1 lb.) of white sugar to every 0.6 litres (1 pint) of juice.

3. Put juice and sugar into the pan and bring to the boil, taking care to stir the sugar away, skimming as the scum arises.

4. After it comes to the boil, boil 5 minutes by the clock and then allow to cool.

5. Stir into each litre (1¾ pints) of juice 0.3 litres (½ pint) of brandy and bottle, corking well.

A measure of these in plain water or soda water is an excellent summer drink. In hot water an excellent night cap for a cold. Mixed in a shaker with a little spirit such as gin — an excellent cocktail.

GINGER BEER
(Urpeth)

Ingredients:—

14 gm tartaric acid	½ oz. tartaric acid
14 gm cream of tartar	½ oz. cream of tartar
14 gm essence of ginger	½ oz. essence of ginger
1 kg sugar	2¼ lbs. sugar
9 litres water	2 galls. water
Yeast nutrient and yeast	Yeast nutrient and yeast

Method:—

1. Put tartaric acid, cream of tartar, ginger essence and sugar into a bowl and pour over 4½ litres (1 gall.) of boiling water. Stir until ingredients are dissolved and add 4½ litres (1 gall.) of cold water.

2. When quite cool stir in the yeast nutrient and yeast.

3. Bottle and tie up securely.

GLEN IRIS HOP BITTERS

Ingredients:—

86 gm hops	3 ozs. hops
30 gm bruised root ginger	1 oz. bruised root ginger
14 gm essence of ginger	½ oz. essence of ginger
1 kg brown sugar	2¼ lbs. brown sugar
14 litres water	3 galls. water
A little honey	A little honey
Yeast	Yeast

Method:—

1. Boil hops, ginger and sugar in 1 litre (1¾ pints) of water gently for 2½ hours, then strain.

2. Then add water to make 14 litres (3 galls). Stir away a little honey and sprinkle the yeast in, giving it a good stir.

3. Stand till cold then bottle.

Point to remember:— Beer must be lukewarm when the yeast is added.

HOME BREWED STOUT

Ingredients:—

0.5 kg black malt	1 lb. black malt
44 gm hops	1½ ozs. hops
58 gm black spanish	2 ozs. black spanish
0.5 kg brown sugar	1 lb. brown sugar
15 litres water	3½ galls. water
Yeast	Yeast

Method:—

1. Stir the malt away in boiling water, add the hops and black spanish and boil for 30 minutes.

2. Strain on to the sugar and stir until the latter is dissolved. Make up to 15 litres (3½ galls.)

3. Stir in the yeast and put into a warm place to ferment for 24 hours, skimming frequently.

4. Pour off carefully leaving the dregs. Bottle and cork tightly.

5. The stout should be ready for use in 4 or 5 days. It improves with keeping.

Point to remember:— The malt can be bought at a chemist's in treacle form.

HONEY BOTCHARD

Ingredients:—

1.5 kg honey	3½ lbs. honey
30 gm hops	1 oz. hops
4.5 litres water	1 gall. water
30 gm yeast	1 oz. yeast
1 slice of toast	1 slice of toast

Method:—

1. Boil the hops in the water for 30 minutes then strain and cool.

2. Stir the honey into the liquid. Spread the yeast on both sides of the toast and float it in the wine and leave to ferment for 21 days. Then skim and bottle.

Yorkshire folk swear by brewer's yeast for making the finest Honey Botchard.

HOP BEER

Ingredients:—

125 gm hops	4 ozs. hops
14 gm bruised root ginger	½ oz. bruised root ginger
1 tablespoonful cracked maize	1 tablespoonful of cracked maize
1.3 kg sugar	3 lbs. sugar
15 litres water	3½ galls. water
58 gm brewer's yeast	2 ozs. brewer's yeast
1 slice of burnt toast	1 slice of burnt toast

Method:—

1. Put the cracked maize with the hops and bruised ginger into a muslin bag.

2. Place in the water and boil until the bag sinks. Lift out the bag and make up the 15 litres (3½ galls.) of water.

3. Stir in the sugar and boil for 5 minutes and strain.

4. When lukewarm add yeast spread on slice of toast. Stand for 3 days, bottle and tie securely.

It will be ready in a fortnight and keeps well for weeks.

Cracked maize can be bought at the poultry food shop.

LEMON GINGER BEER
(For Haytime)

Ingredients:—

58 gm bruised root ginger	2 ozs. bruised root ginger
58 gm cream of tartar	2 ozs. cream of tartar
1.3 kg sugar	3 lbs. sugar
9 litres boiling water	2 galls. boiling water
3 lemons	3 lemons
30 gm brewer's yeast	1 oz. brewer's yeast
1 slice of toast	1 slice of toast

Method:—

1. Peel the lemon rinds thinly and squeeze out the juice. Put with the sugar, bruised ginger and cream of tartar in a large bucket and pour over the whole of the boiling water.

2. When lukewarm mix a little of the beer with the yeast and spread it over the toast and lay it on the top of the brew. Let it ferment 24 hours, then strain and bottle, corking securely.

ORANGE GIN

Ingredients:—

6 Seville oranges	6 Seville oranges
2½ lemons	2½ lemons
0.7 kg loaf sugar	1½ lbs. loaf sugar
3 bottles of best unsweetened gin	3 bottles of best unsweetened gin

Method:—

1. Peel the fruit thinly (that is just taking off the yellow rind) and put peel, sugar and gin into a jar.
2. Shake up each day for 14 days, then strain and bottle.

PARSLEY BRANDY

Ingredients:—

250 gm parlsey	½ lb. parsley
14 gm bruised root ginger	½ ox. bruised root ginger
1.5 kg sugar	3½ lbs. sugar
4.5 litres water	1 gall. water
1 tablespoonful of raisins	1 tablespoonful of raisins
2 oranges and 2 lemons	2 oranges and 2 lemons
Tannin, yeast nutrient and yeast	Tannin, yeast nutrient and yeast

Method:—

1. Wash the parsley and add it to the water. Boil for 30 minutes, then strain and throw away the parsley.
2. Put the thinly pared rinds of the oranges and lemons together with the sugar and root ginger into a polythene bucket. Pour on the boiling water and stir until the sugar is dissolved.
3. Allow to cool then add the juice from the fruit and take a hydrometer reading.
4. Add tannin, yeast nutrient, yeast and chopped raisins and ferment.

RASPBERRY VINEGAR

Ingredients:—

1 litre vinegar	1¼ pints vinegar
1 litre raspberries	1¼ pints raspberries
Allow 0.5 kg of sugar to 0.6 litres of juice	Allow 1 lb. of sugar to 1 pint of juice

Method:—

1. Put the vinegar in a bowl and add the raspberries as you gather them (if you have just a few bushes) until you have sufficient.

2. Squeeze and mash every day for 9 days, then strain and press through a nylon bag.

3. Measure the juice, add the sugar and bring to the boil and then boil only 5 minutes by the clock.

4. Fine on rice or plain suet pudding and for a summer's drink with cold water. With hot water a fine remedy for a cold.

RED ROB

Ingredients:—

Ripe elderberries	Ripe elderberries
Water	Water
To every 0.6 litres of juice:—	To every 1 pint of juice:—
0.5 kg sugar	1 lb. sugar
To every 2 litres of juice:—	To every 3½ pints of juice:—
14 gm cassia buds	½ oz. cassia buds
14 gm bruised root ginger	½ oz. bruised root ginger
14 gm whole cloves	½ oz. whole cloves

Method:—

1. Strip the elderberries from the stalks and just cover them with water. Simmer for 20 minutes until all the juice is in the water, then strain.

2. Measure and add the sugar, cassia buds, ginger and cloves, and boil very gently for another 5 minutes. You must be careful or it will jelly.

3. A measure in hot water or in a glass of mulled ale is fine as a night cap on a cold night.

RHUBARB-APRICOT WHISKY

Ingredients:—

3 kg rhubarb	6½ lbs. rhubarb
1 kg dried apricots	2¼ lbs. dried apricots
1.7 kg sugar	4 lbs. sugar
4.5 litres water	1 gall. water
2 Campden tablets	2 Campden tablets
Tannin, yeast nutrient and yeast	Tannin, yeast nutrient and yeast

Method:—

1. Soak the apricots in the cold water overnight then boil them gently until very tender. Strain from the water and use the apricots.

2. Cut up the rhubarb and add it to the apricot water which must be made up to 4½ litres (1 gall.). Put in the crushed Campden tablets and leave for 14 days, stirring often, then strain.

3. Add the sugar to the strained liquid and stir until it is dissolved. Take a reading with the hydrometer.

4. Put in the tannin, yeast nutrient and yeast and ferment.

RHUBARB BAKE WHISKY

Ingredients:—

0.5 kg bread	1 lb. bread
3 kg rhubarb	6½ lbs. rhubarb
1.7 kg white sugar	4 lbs. white sugar
4.5 litres cold water	1 gall. cold water
2 Campden tablets	2 Campden tablets
Tannin, yeast nutrient and yeast	Tannin, yeast nutrient and yeast

Method:—

1. Cut the bread into slices and toast it a nice brown both sides — but on no account burn or this spoils the flavour entirely.

2. Put into a polythene bucket with the cold water and the crushed Campden tablets. Cut up the rhubarb and add. Leave to mash for 9 days, stirring often and squeezing the toast with the hand, then strain and throw away the pulp

3. Add the sugar and stir until it is dissolved. Take a reading with the hydrometer.

4. Put in the tannin, yeast nutrient and yeast and ferment.

RHUBARB BRANDY
(A White Wine)

Ingredients:—

2.7 kg rhubarb	6 lbs. rhubarb
250 gm large raisins	½ lb. large raisins
1.7 kg white sugar	4 lbs. white sugar
4.5 litres cold water	1 gall. cold water
4 egg shells	4 egg shells
2 Campden tablets	2 Campden tablets
Tannin, yeast nutrient and yeast	Tannin, yeast nutrient and yeast

Method:—

1. Peel all the green and red off the rhubarb then cut it up small and weigh. Put into a polythene bucket, cover with the water and add the crushed Campden tablets and the chopped raisins. Allow to stand 10-14 days, stirring and squeezing the fruit every day. Strain and throw away the pulp.

2. Add the egg shells, crushed to pieces, and the sugar and stir to dissolve the latter. Take a hyrometer reading.

3. Put in the tannin, yeast nutrient and yeast and ferment.

RHUBARB COCKTAIL
(A Fine Rich Wine)

Ingredients:—

1 kg mixed dried fruit	2¼ lbs. mixed dried fruit
6 kg rhubarb	13 lbs. rhubarb
2 kg sugar	4½ lbs. sugar
4.5 litres water	1 gall. water
4 Campden tablets	4 Campden tablets
Tannin, yeast nutrient and yeast	Tannin, yeast nutrient and yeast

Method:—

1. Soak the dried fruit in the water overnight, then bring to the boil and simmer until tender. Strain out the fruit and use as food. Make the water up to 4½ litres (1 gall.).

2. Cut up one half of the rhubarb and put it in the fruit water together with 2 crushed Campden tablets. Stir often and leave to stand for 1 week. Squeeze out all the rhubarb pulp and then add the remaining rhubarb, also cut up small, and the remaining 2 crushed tablets. Let it stand another week then squeeze out all the pulp.

3. Add the sugar and stir until dissolved. Take a reading with the hydrometer.

4. Put in the tannin, yeast nutrient and yeast and ferment.

RHUBARB WHISKY (1)

Ingredients:—

3 kg rhubarb	6½ lbs. rhubarb
0.7 kg wheat	1½ lbs. wheat
0.5 kg raisins	1 lb. raisins
1.7 kg Demerara sugar	4 lbs. Demerara sugar
4.5 litres cold water	1 gall. cold water
2 Campden tablets	2 Campden tablets
2 egg shells	2 egg shells
4 lemons	4 lemons
Tannin, yeast nutrient and yeast	Tannin, yeast nutrient and yeast

Method:—

1. Cut the rhubarb up small and cover it with cold water. Add the wheat and the crushed Campden tablets and leave to mash for 10-14 days, stirring often. Strain and squeeze all the moisture out of the pulp before throwing it away.

2. Strain the liquid through a fine nylon bag. Add the sugar, chopped raisins, crushed egg shells and the juice and thinly pared rinds of the lemons. Stir well and take a hydrometer reading.

3. Put in the tannin, yeast nutrient and yeast and ferment.

RHUBARB WHISKY (2)

Ingredients:—

3 kg rhubarb	6½ lbs. rhubarb
125 gm large raisins	¼ lb. large raisins
1.5 kg sugar	3½ lbs. sugar
4.5 litres water	1 gall. water
1 egg shell	1 egg shell
1 lemon	1 lemon
2 Campden tablets	2 Campden tablts
Tannin, yeast nutrient and yeast	Tannin, yeast nutrient and yeast

Method:—

1. Cut up the rhubarb small and cover with cold water. Put in the crushed Campden tablets and let it stand for 10-14 days stirring daily.

2. Strain off the liquid and add the raisins, well chopped, the crushed egg shell, sugar and the juice and thinly pared rind of the lemon. Stir to dissolve the sugar and take a hydrometer reading.

3. Put in the tannin, yeast nutrient and yeast and ferment.

SLOE GIN
(Alnwick)

Ingredients:—

1.5 kg ripe sloes (November)	3 lbs. ripe sloes (November)
2 litres unsweetened gin	3½ pints unsweetened gin
0.7 kg crushed sugar candy (brown)	1½ lbs. crushed sugar candy (brown)
14 gm bitter almonds	½ oz. bitter almonds
6 cloves	6 cloves

Method:—

1. Prick the sloes all over with a silver plated fork.

2. Put them into a large jar or bottle, add the sugar candy, gin, cloves and chopped almonds.

3. Shake it every day for a month then occasionally for another month, then strain and bottle.

STRAWBERRY VINEGAR

Ingredients:—

1 litre white vinegar	1¾ pints white vinegar
1 litre strawberries	1¾ pints strawberries
Allow 0.5 kg of sugar to 0.6 litres of juice	Allow 1 lb. of sugar to 1 pint of juice

Method:—

1. Put the vinegar into a large bowl and add the strawberries. Let them stand 6 days, while you press and squeeze them daily. Then strain off the juice through a nylon bag and press out until the pulp is dry.

2. Measure and add the sugar then bring to the boil and boil gently for 5 minutes. You must be careful to time the boiling or the vinegar will jelly.

TONIC STOUT

Ingredients:—

1.5 kg parsnips	3½ lbs. parsnips
58 gm hops	2 ozs. hops
125 gm brown malt (as bought in treacle form at the chemist's)	¼ lb. brown malt (as bought in treacle form at the chemist's)
1 kg sugar	2¼ lbs. sugar
4.5 litres water	1 gall. water
30 gm brewer's yeast	1 oz. brewer's yeast

Method:—

1. Clean and boil the parsnips in one half of the water until they are tender. Strain the water.

2. Boil the hops in the other half of the water for 15 minutes, then strain.

3. Add the two waters together, stir away in it the sugar and malt and leave until lukewarm.

4. Sprinkle the yeast on top and leave two days then bottle. Do not cork tightly or you will have explosions.